Master Your Mind

Master Your Success

HOW TO EMPOWER YOUR THOUGHTS,
OVERCOME PROCRASTINATION, ACHIEVE YOUR
GOALS AND LIVE A LIFE ON YOUR TERMS

MARK DALTON

Thank you to my amazing family for your support, wisdom, guidance and most importantly, Your LOVE.

TABLE OF CONTENTS

INTRODUCTION

There is nothing greater than achieving an enormous goal. The early mornings, the late nights, the sacrifices, the mistakes, the failures and most importantly, the commitment to push on when every inch of your body is telling you to STOP.

I have experienced this many times, and it certainly takes you out of your comfort zone. Your mindset plays a huge part in your ability to absorb the pressures that comes with stretching yourself. I want to share the strategies and principles that will fast track your ability to achieve your goals faster than ever before!

I will show you that with just simple daily actions implemented into your current schedule and with small incremental changes, you can achieve the life-changing goals that you deserve. What I'm about to show you will prove that with the right goal-setting structure, correct supportive habits and a changed mindset, you can achieve everything you set your mind to.

This is, *Master Your Mind – Master Your Success.*

My name is Mark Dalton, and I want to provide you with all the knowledge to help transform how you set your goals, develop supportive habits and change your mindset to achieve greatness.

To provide you with some details of my background, I am a former elite athlete, specializing in middle distance events. I have a significant wealth of experience in health, fitness and wellbeing. I have a Bachelor of Physical Education & Health and I am a qualified Personal Trainer and sports coach. I have competed in the National Championships for athletics and continue to coach and train young athletes.

I have complimented my sporting achievements with an extensive employment career having served on several Executive Teams. I am also the Founder of a Personal & Business Consultancy firm. My personal experience has provided me with the opportunity to share all that I have learned to help you with establishing goals and supportive daily habits.

How this book will help you

I wrote *Master Your Mind – Master Your Success* to let you know what separates the high achievers from the average achievers and what it will take to reach the top of your game.

Master Your Mind – Master Your Success is all about providing you with a set of principles, habits, goals, structures, beliefs, a new mindset and a clear vision for what you need to do. With only 3% of adults having clear and written goals, it is time for you to separate yourself from the other 97% of people and create some definite results.

Many people have completely transformed their lives in less than a year from the systems I will show you in this book, and you would be astounded with how some decisions and actions – be that good or bad – can completely change your journey. At any time, the choices we make are either moving us closer or further away from our goals. We are either helping or hindering our chances of success and fulfilment, but you may be just one amazing decision or choice away from a life-altering moment.

'The actions we take and the decisions we make will impact where we are in 12 months, three years or even 30 years.'

I want you to appreciate that your journey is different from every other human, and I want you to live your life to its fullest potential. I don't think there's ever a reason to live an average life. If you have been reluctant to take the right actions to achieve your goals, you have come to the right place. I will show you the steps to take daily action to extract everything out of life that you can. I know you are ready to make a huge difference in your life and the way you have been living. You may be already well on your way, and this book will provide the reassurance that you are on the right track. For others, this book could completely reprogram your mindset and will be the moment that completely transforms your life. I want this to be the exact moment that things change for you.

MASTER SUCCESS PRINCIPLE #1

THE POWER OF VISUALIZATION AND GOAL SETTING

Take a look around you. Everything you see that wasn't created by nature over millions of years was in the very beginning just a thought, a dream or a vision of a person and then slowly, steps were taken to make it a reality. The clothes you are wearing, the bed you sleep in, the chair you sit on, the shoes you are wearing, the blinds on the windows or even the reading glasses on your face were all just an initial idea developed in the imagination. To bring these to life, small steps and daily actions were taken to bring the initial thought to reality. You see, with the right thinking, your brain doesn't have any limitations. It's the most advanced supercomputer in the world. It's so advanced that we've only scratched the surface of its capabilities and perhaps we will never have a complete understanding of its power.

When you imagine yourself achieving something and attach feelings to it, your brain automatically kicks into action at a subconscious level. If you develop your visualization, so it feels like it's reality, your mind will start to provide you with the ideas, suggestions and intuition to allow you to see those opportunities that bring you closer to your goals. Some people call these events a 'coincidence', but there is something much bigger at play that we still don't fully understand. It's an energy source that flows and is in constant motion. You would've heard the saying "I have a gut feeling about this", or to listen to your 'intuition'. Well, there's scientific evidence to prove that your heart actually has brain cells, 40,000 neurons and 100,000 times the electrical charge of any other organ in the body, and the gut actually has neurological tissue! In eastern science, they suggest we have three brains: the head brain, the heart brain and the gut-brain. All of these organs are much more closely linked to our thoughts and feelings than we had ever first imagined.

Trusting Your Intuition

It can be very challenging to trust your 'intuition' or 'gut feeling', but it's actually providing you with the answers that allow you to take the necessary daily steps to achieve your goals and guide you on life's journey. It may cognitively feel at times that you are being guided down a particular path to make a decision, but when you reflect on it many years down the track, you can appreciate why you followed that journey.

Sometimes we feel that a particular decision we've made is wrong or has caused us to be derailed from our journey. In fact, you will realize that if you view this decision as a 'learning opportunity', you will become much stronger for the experience and another opportunity will become evident if you stay focused, determined and are prepared to stay the course, regardless of the battle scars you may receive. The sooner you realize that your 'path' contains obstacles, challenges and setbacks, the sooner you will accept it as a learning opportunity. At the time, it's difficult to understand why the event has occurred. However, the universe has a unique way of correcting your journey so that things happen *for* you, and not *to* you.

You need to expect that the bigger your goals, the bigger the challenges and the greater the setbacks you are likely to face. It's like the universe is throwing you constant challenges to test your capacity to absorb, weave and negotiate your path. There will be times that really test your resilience, your faith, your courage, your leadership and your mental strength. Each of us is impacted differently by challenges, but it's not what you are dealt with in life, it's how you deal with it that will make you stand out from the crowd.

The Importance of the Subconscious

Daily visualization exercises will greatly assist you on the path to success. If you are going to plant the seeds into your subconscious mind, you might as well imagine the perfect life. I'd much rather get close to achieving a **BIG** goal and just miss than achieve a small goal that doesn't propel me forward. Remember, you are only limited by your beliefs, so if you aim for *average*, then you will visualize achieving the small things. You end up attracting average opportunities, you won't progress, and your momentum will be slow. If you want to live a spectacular life and attract the 'blow your mind' kind of opportunities, then set the bar high. Don't get this confused with achieving small daily goals on your way to achieving the **BIGGER** ones. We'll cover that later on, but here's a great example of goals and visualization.

A world-class high jumper can only jump to their maximum when the bar is set really high. These days, we're talking over 2.3m! If the bar was set at 1.1m, there's no way the high jumper will be able to jump 2.3m without having the bar nice and high to focus on. If you have ever watched a world-class athlete in the high jump, part of their routine is to visualize. They close their eyes and can see the whole jump by using their arms and legs to motion the technique. Prior to the competition, the high jumper has visualized clearing the bar thousands of times before. They've felt the energy of the crowd, the run-up, the take-off, arching their back, the clearance of their legs, and the elation and celebration as they softly land on the mat. I'm sure in many instances, it's a 'déjà vu' event for the athlete given the strength of their visualization and focus on the outcome.

Planting the dream seed isn't just a once-off occurrence, and that's where people get it wrong when initially writing down their goals. Planting the dream seed should become a daily visualization experience that enables you to embed the dream seed further into your mind. You can think of it like planting a seed in the ground during summer. Without regular attention such as watering, the seed won't start to grow, and the weeds (other thoughts) start to take over. However, if you regularly water, fertilize and nurture your seed, it will gain strength, the roots will push down into the soil providing support and strength, and your seed will start to form into a mature plant.

Assignment Task

What does a daily visualization activity look like?

Your assignment for today is to put into practice what I'm about to teach you. It will form a great structure for your daily visualization to embed your dream seed (goal) into your subconscious.

Step One: You will need to have a peaceful soundtrack that allows you to drift into a deep calmness. I have two soundtracks that I use, which I recorded myself. One is of the ocean, and the other is of a small running stream. I recorded both sounds at two very special locations to me, so I engage in instant relaxation whenever I hear the sounds. If you do record your own, they need to be no longer than 15-20 minutes. In the last 60 seconds of the recording, you can say very quietly and almost in a whisper: "I want you to now take three deep breaths and slowly open your eyes – your visualization will be complete in 60 seconds."

Step Two: Once you have your recorded sound, you need to find a quiet, comfortable and relaxing location. This could be in a favorite chair, but I recommend not flat on your back in a bed. Sitting upright is preferable. Use a quality pair of headphones for sound quality and if required, a blanket during winter to keep warm.

Step Three: When comfortable, start your soundtrack and close your eyes. Have both your feet positioned flat on the ground and your hands resting gently on your thighs. Take five slow, deep and rhythmic breaths initially, by breathing in through your nose and out through your mouth. On the last two breaths, *say the following to yourself* by breathing in and out through your mouth:

Breath 1: "Breathing in quality, breathing out mediocrity."

Breath 2: "Breathing in strength, breathing out weakness."

Step Four: During the initial five minutes, it's all about getting the 'noise' out of your mind. Some feel like they fail at the traditional meditation experience because they can't quieten the mind to 'outer noise'. This is where I find the adapted visualization exercise better suited for many people, as they can bring to focus their 'future self' rather than quieten their mind completely. If you feel other thoughts coming in, just quietly take 2-3 very gentle, shallow breaths and say to yourself "out with the noise, in with the quiet."

Step Five: During your visualization, you are to focus on a special goal of yours that you want to achieve. Try and focus on a single goal rather than too many. I want you to use the following guiding questions to help you focus. You need to feel like you are already in the moment and have achieved your goal.

- Where are you going to be?
- Where specifically is the location?
- Who are you going to be with?
- What sounds can you hear?
- What are the conversations you are having?
- What can you smell?
- What are you touching? Can you feel the different surfaces and textures?

Step Six: For the final 60 seconds, take three deep breaths and slowly open your eyes. Smile and say: "Today is going to be a great day, and I'm another step closer to achieving my goals."

Optional Step.

Following my visualization, I like to participate in some creative thinking for 5-10 minutes. When you participate in the visualization as per the steps above, you start using different parts of your mind that are usually suppressed in normal everyday activities. It's when you are able to calm your mind and become relaxed that some of the most creative ideas begin to flow.

I have a notepad close by, just gently close my eyes and plant an idea or problem that I might have, and I begin the problem-solving process. As the ideas begin to come, I start to write them down on my notepad. You will be amazed at the creative ideas you come up with when you are in this state of mind.

Where do you want to be in one, three, five or even 20 years?

We're often told to 'live in the now', but I'd like to challenge that mentality. Yes, we need to enjoy every day on this amazing planet but without looking into the future, how can we challenge and commit ourselves today if we don't know what we want tomorrow? Where can you see yourself in one year, three years, five years or even 20 years?

Some may think we have a set predetermined life that we're just playing out; a bit like a movie script. I think we have multiple scripts that we can choose from, and they're hidden via 'opportunities' that pass by every single day.

'The vision you SEE is up to ME.'

Casting your vision forward to where you want to be in one year, let alone ten years can initially be challenging. It's hard enough to cast our mind back to what we were doing ten years ago, let alone what we wish to achieve ten years into the future.

Creating a clear vision is so important, be it through daydreaming, meditation or deliberate focus activities. Throughout the following lessons, I'm going to provide you with the tools required to build the life you wish to lead and importantly, build the blueprint plan to get you there.

THE 8 STEPS TO GOALS SETTING

Without ACTION, nothing ever happens. If there is one single phrase that I want you to remember from this book, please let it be this: "The decisions you MAKE and the actions you TAKE will define your SUCCESS." You can read all the self-help books, attend as many seminars, conferences, listen to podcasts, enroll in online courses but without taking that knowledge and putting it into practice then you will remain idle. What separates the high achievers from the low achievers, the rich versus the poor, an influencer to a follower, simply comes down to the decisions you make and the actions you take, as they will define the path you carve towards your ultimate success.

"The decisions you MAKE and the actions you TAKE will define your SUCCESS."
Mark Dalton

STEP 1.
CLARITY - DREAM BIG. Get clarity on what you want.

STEP 2.
PERSONAL - Make it personal and relevant

STEP 3.
TAKE ACTION - Take immediate action and write up your BIG goals

STEP 4.
PLAN - Develop your plan and actions

STEP 5.
TIME - Develop specific and realistic time frames for your goals

STEP 6.
COMMITMENT - Follow through with your commitment and start

STEP 7.
OPPORTUNITY - Be observant of opportunities that present

STEP 8.

START – Do not procrastinate. Get started today and take action

CLARITY

As humans, we have such a unique opportunity to dream and visualize a future existence; one that is yet to take place, but one whereby we can generate the feelings of what that future existence will be through the excretion of hormones from our brain. We can close our eyes and even create the sounds and conversations we hear, the people we are with and the things we will touch, all with the most incredible detail.

I'd like you to put this into practice by reading the following short paragraph and then closing your eyes. You will most likely start to visualize the scenery as you read the description, but I want you to relive the experience and make it incredibly detailed by gently closing your eyes and taking three very slow, deep and controlled breaths.

Imagine yourself walking along a gravel path towards the beautiful ocean. You come to the end of the path, where there are three wooden steps leading

down to the sand. You stop, hold onto the smooth timber railing and your eyes focus out towards the beautiful glistening ocean. You take a slow, deep breath in through your nose and you can smell the salt air. You gently look left and right, and there's not a soul to be seen, apart from a flock of seagulls by the water's edge, scurrying up and down the tideline as the foam of the water washes up onto the sand.

The waves are only small, but the gentle sound they make is so peaceful. You slip off your shoes and hold them in your right hand, and then you slide your left hand down the pine railing. It's extremely smooth from the years of being weathered by the wind, the rain and the hot sun. You take three steps down to the sand, and it's so nice and warm under the soles of your feet. You bend down and take a handful of warm sand. You open up your hand and let the sand filter back out through your fingers as it drifts away with the ocean breeze. You look back out to the ocean again, and you can hear the seagulls chirping away to each other. You drop your shoes and raise both your arms towards the sky and tilt your head back, taking in the beautiful sunshine.

The first stage of your goal setting is to use your imagination and your visualization skills to think of the things you really want to achieve. Be bold and think big. The goals you want to achieve need to stretch you and will drive you every day. They are the things that will push you through the challenging times, and you need to have a strong enough attachment to the goals that will aid your resilience and guide you through the problems and obstacles you will face.

Dreaming big doesn't mean being unrealistic. There's no point dreaming of being an NBA basketballer for the Chicago Bulls if you are 5'5" and 35 years old. It's just simply unattainable. Wanting to have a million dollars in your bank account, on the other hand, is realistic, depending on the 'realistic' timeframe you allow. The initial dreaming doesn't require anything more than having some quiet time to yourself and to think of the next 12 months, or even the next ten years. It's your opportunity to simply visualize and think broadly, then attach a reason or your purpose towards each of the goals you'd like to achieve.

PERSONAL

The relevance of your goals needs to be specifically what YOU want and not for somebody else. Sure, your goals can have a positive impact on others, but the actual goal itself needs to be your idea and yours alone. It needs to be relevant to you because you need to be driven and have a healthy obsession towards achieving your goal. What will this goal mean to you when you achieve it? What positive impact will it have for you and perhaps those that will benefit from the goal being achieved? Your goal will require small, regular and tangible actions, stepping you towards your goal. This will require an ongoing commitment and energy; therefore, the relevance is even more important. Take ownership of your goals, and they need to be yours and yours alone.

TAKE ACTION

Once you have taken the time to dream up your goals, the next step is to take immediate ACTION. This is not a time for procrastination, because writing down your goals is what I call 'inking your goal tattoo', which we'll cover in the next chapter. The process of writing down your goals is the initial development stage for your subconscious. Think of it as the contract that you make with yourself to become accountable for your goals. Without you taking action at this step, you should never expect anything to change. As they say, if you don't change, nothing will change!

PLAN

Think of this part like you were the captain of a ship. You wouldn't leave the safe waters of the bay to travel across treacherous seas without carefully planning the voyage. Yes, there could be changes in your course due to unforeseen storms, rough seas or weather conditions, but that's life! You can never predict the challenges you will face as you navigate your own journey towards your goals. Your destination map will contain many different voyages, with no two the same. Some days the wind will be in your sails, while others will feel like you have got a serious headwind, blowing you backwards or even off course. You must ride out the rough conditions, enjoy the times when the seas are smooth, and soon enough, you will see the endpoint in the distance and celebrate achieving your goals.

TIME

Time is the fifth step, making sure your goals are very time-focused and specific but realistic. Your brain is so switched on that it automatically comes up with your personal time schedule without too much conscious thought, as it has a clear understanding of an endpoint (time).

By placing a specific date against your goals, you can then begin to develop a similar plan around what needs to be achieved over a certain timeframe. You can then set the speed for your journey and complete the required actions. There's no point staying in first gear and working at a snail's pace if your goal is to run a half marathon in three months, but you have got no training schedule prepared and have no base level of fitness. For something like this, you'd better get cracking and develop your schedule, arrange coaching if required and begin your training immediately. You will need to move from first gear to fifth gear very quickly to build your fitness and strength, so you can meet the demands of a half marathon.

The time allocated to a goal helps us to subconsciously prioritize actions that we need to complete the goal. On many occasions, one goal will lend itself to moving closer towards another goal, therefore to keep on track, we need to complete one of our 12-month goals before we can move closer to a five-year goal. For example, if a five-year goal was to have three investment properties, year one would be to take the required steps to purchase property number one. If you keep delaying the purchase of your first property until year three, purchasing the second and third properties in the remaining two years will become much more challenging and place unwarranted pressure on you.

A timeframe against your goal will keep you accountable, and help you to establish the plans, coordinates and daily micro-actions that need to occur for your goal to be achieved. An endpoint keeps you moving forward and anchors you to the specific timeline, so you can prepare to celebrate as you achieve your goal.

COMMITMENT

This is when you finally lift the safety seal that covers the switch to launch. Three... two... one... and it's GO time! The implementation phase gets your momentum moving forward, and this is when the magic really begins. For so many people, if they can move into the implementation phase and make that commitment towards following their plan, they have a huge chance of reaching their goal – or goals – as long as they stay true to the course. Just take that first step which so many people fail to do.

OPPORTUNITY

Opportunities are always passing by, but it's up to each of us to seize those moments. If you don't take your opportunity, the universe has an uncanny way of passing them onto someone else! The *opportunity* component is all about awareness. When you review your goals on a regular basis, you subconsciously become more aware of those opportunities that will assist you to continue with your forward momentum.

Opportunities can present themselves in all sorts of weird and wonderful ways. It could be a chance meeting on the street with someone you haven't seen for five years, and that person has a key connection with someone that really needs your services. It could be an advertisement in the newspaper for a seminar regarding property investment (one of your goals) from a well-regarded and experienced person. This particular expert might only visit your region or country once every few years; therefore, if you don't take up this opportunity, you may miss out on some excellent guidance and advice for future property investment to tick off one of your goals.

You may think that some opportunities have happened by luck or by 'pure chance', however, you need to have an awareness of what you need to look out for. If an opportunity does present, it also comes down to taking action. If it requires a conversation, a follow-up phone call or emails, then do it. Don't wait for a couple of days: act immediately and get on the front foot. Too many people procrastinate when presented with an amazing opportunity. Make a decision and act on it; otherwise, you will find that another 'lucky' person grabs the opportunity and does something with it. I often hear of people saying "I came up with that invention two years ago, and now that person's a multi-millionaire!" Well, don't be frustrated, you had the opportunity to do something about it, and you didn't, so act on it when presented next time and do something about it.

START

The final step is to START NOW. You have completed the seven steps to get to this point, and it's your time to put them all into action and do it now! There's no better time than the present to use your momentum and take this opportunity to implement your goal setting into your life. It will take significant ongoing commitment, daily structure, planning, courage and tackling your limiting beliefs with ferocity because you have developed your goals for a reason and therefore that reason needs to be strong and powerful.

The next chapter will further broaden your understanding of the goal-setting process and clearly identify why each of the areas is fundamentally linked.

MASTER SUCCESS PRINCIPLE #2

IT STARTS WITH A PLAN

Think BIG

There's a very popular saying: "Aim for the moon, and you might just hit the stars." Basically, setting big goals will allow you to achieve so much more than not setting them at all. Even if you don't manage to achieve your ultimate goal, you will be significantly closer than not setting any goals at all. In many circumstances, the goal might not just be achieved, but smashed out of the park!

> **"We greatly overestimate what we can do in one year but greatly underestimate what is possible for us in five years."**
> Peter Drucker

It's important that we initially start with a mighty big goal, not an outrageous goal and then take the small actionable steps to work our way along that journey to achieve it. You shouldn't hold back on what you'd like to achieve. If you are holding back on thinking BIG, is it because you think that it's unattainable or is there possibly a fear that you need to overcome?

There's a big difference though to being unrealistic with goal setting. It would be unrealistic to put down a goal to win an Olympic gold medal in the pole vault if you are in your mid-30s and don't have the physical attributes to compete with the world's best. There's a difference between dreaming big and being unrealistic with goal setting. The only 'unrealistic' limitation you can have is the time you wish to achieve the goal by.

When thinking BIG, it's okay to include big-ticket items like a dream car, owning a beach holiday house or having $1 million in the bank. But be mindful that they may only give you short-term euphoria and not fulfilment, love and ongoing happiness. It's fine to want these things, and that's completely your decision, but what I would really encourage you to do with the majority of your goals is to think carefully about those that will bring ongoing happiness that you can share with your loved ones, and not just material items like expensive cars, boats and jewelry. Doing something only for short-term financial gain is on the very low end of the scale when it comes to maintaining your motivation and commitment, so be sure you think carefully of what you want. Dreaming provides you with no boundaries and unlimited possibilities. The stronger the dream, the stronger the connection and energy you will have towards achieving your goal to remain focused over your journey. Without a goal, the things you want in the future are purely hopes and wishes.

Inking Your Goal Tattoo

Writing down your goals is your way of etching the 'goal tattoo' into your mind. The Basil Ganglia is a part of our brain that plays a key role in the development of our memories, development of emotions and pattern behavior for goal setting. We, therefore, need to ensure that by writing down the goal and creating your 'visualization tattoo', that whenever you read your goals out loud or look at your 'dream board', it sends a stimuli message to our Basil Ganglia to keep producing the required subconscious messages. If the stimuli aren't refreshed frequently, our brain starts to focus on other tasks that it feels may be more of a priority.

Goal-setting visualization is about relaxing, dreaming, fueling your commitment and focusing on what your future life will look like. It needs to feel like it's in real-time, crystal clear and repeated each day. The best way I can describe it would be to imagine the most amazing movie you have ever seen. The clarity of the picture is like nothing you have seen before, and you can touch and smell the objects or items, and see the people with you. You need to be able to hear the sounds in that very moment and visualize that you have everything you want in your life.

Assignment Task

I know from experience that when an action item comes up, you tend to skip through it and keep moving forward. Well, this is different because as I've mentioned throughout the academy so far, it's all about taking immediate ACTION. If you skip this section and keep reading on, it will have the single biggest negative impact on your chances of achieving success. I repeat, your single biggest negative impact – so this Assignment task is compulsory and not discretionary.

Writing Down Your Goals

Get out a brand-new spiral notebook and place on the top of the page 'My 12 Month Goals' and today's date. Please don't use a computer to record your goals. The physical process of handwriting your goals etches the goal into your subconscious so it can get to work.

Next, start to note down every goal you want to achieve that's relevant to you over the next 12 months but place them in the past tense like you have already achieved the goal. E.g. I have travelled to Switzerland for an amazing family holiday, or I have read 20 books this year.

As we've discussed during this chapter, it is important to have balance in your goal setting across the key areas of Health, Wealth, Self & Happiness. If your preference is to use a goal setting template, please refer to the free gift that I offer and use the templates I've developed. Remember, for each of your goals; you need to have a 'reason' or your 'why' for wanting to achieve the goal, along with a timeline or date that you want to achieve the goal by.

Next, place a tick beside the TOP 10 Goals you would like to achieve over the next 12 months and use a blank A4 piece of paper to re-write your Top 10 Goals and read over them.

Once you have completed the 12-month goals, start a fresh page and write down your 5 – 10 Year Goals. Again, write down every single goal you can think of that you would like to achieve. Don't hold back and ensure you think BIG!

To assist, please refer to the following guiding questions:

Health goals – guiding questions:
- What will I do to stay fit?
- What exercise should I incorporate into my daily schedule?
- What is the frequency of exercise per week?

Wealth goals – guiding questions:
- Where do I want to be living?
- What investments do I want to own?
- Is there a savings or financial goal I want to achieve?

Self and Happiness goals – guiding questions:
- What career do I want to be in, or do I want to start my own business?
- How many books do I want to read or what skills do I want to improve in?
- Is there a holiday or destination I wish to travel to?
- Do you have a relationship goal?
- Is there a goal you wish to make towards your community?

- Is there a special item you wish to purchase as a reward for achieving your goals?
- What one skill do you need to become great at that would completely change your life?

GOAL 1
REASON for this goal? (Your WHY)
Time Frame (Date)
GOAL 2
REASON for this goal? (Your WHY)
Time Frame (Date)
GOAL 3
REASON for this goal? (Your WHY)
Time Frame (Date)

Developing Your Plan

We're often bombarded with podcasts, TV shows and various books talking about the importance of goal-setting strategies. I'm a *huge* advocate of this important first step of setting goals, but many are led to believe that once you have set your goals and noted them down (if you are lucky), the magic will just start to happen! The 'average' person will make a so-called New Year's resolution and promise to get that new job, start their own business or even shed some weight. Gyms absolutely *love* these kinds of people, and they have thousands of members that join up in January each year with all the right intentions, only to give up attending because the first few workouts made their muscles ache. In short, it wasn't a 'sustainable' kind of exercise, and they never set the right daily habits and structures to commit to their long-term goal and didn't build the foundations slowly.

Initial visualization

The initial visualization of your *BIG goals* forms the very start of the journey. Every part of that journey would have been mapped out to reach that ULTIMATE GOAL. For the average person, they fail to understand that the initial visualization and goal setting forms just *5 %* of the whole process. For some, they stop there and check-in at dream island.

Relevance

Importantly, make your goals relevant to YOU. There's no point aiming to achieve the goals of others. You need to take complete ownership of the goals and have the passion and drive to achieve them, and to have a 'REASON' for your goal. Why is it that you want to achieve that goal? You need to be emotionally connected to the goal so that you take small actions each day towards achieving it.

Taking Action

The third step of the process is to take ACTION and write your goals down. I'll repeat: please write your goals down. This is part of the 'goal tattoo' process that I mentioned earlier in this chapter, which forms a huge part of developing your subconscious to seek out the path and bring to your attention the opportunities that allow you to move closer to your goal. It's amazing how many more so-called 'coincidences' start to occur when you have set your goals.

When you initially start writing down your goals, you might come up with pages of things you'd like to achieve. When you have done that, begin to narrow your focus on your top 10 goals for the next 12 months. You want to avoid such a broad focus where it all appears to be overwhelming, and you are flicking through page after page, not knowing where to start. Your initial goals should be ones that will give you *the confidence* to build a foundation along with supporting daily habits, and a checkpoint to know you are on target for your long-term (10-year) ultimate goal.

The Plan

The fourth step is to develop your *plan* to achieve your goals. This is where many people miss the mark on goal setting. Many are led to believe that once you write down your goals, you can place them on your wall or place them in an envelope and forget about them. This is a sure-fire way to significantly limit the opportunity to achieve your goal. I'll cover off 'checkpoints' soon.

The final step includes the implementation phase, keeping an eye out for opportunities and living in the NOW.

Here is an outline of how long you should spend on each area for goal setting.

(% = time allocated to the task)

5%: Initial development of your goals, what you want to achieve, and WHY? It's your time to dream.

10%: Writing your goals down and narrowing the focus to a top five. Include a date to achieve.

15%: Development of your 'destination map';

establishing your coordinates and knowing what the end goal will look like.

10%: Daily visualization, writing out your top 10 goals and reading them out loud

20%: Establishing daily habits to take you closer to your goals each day. Write down 2-3 things each day that you need to action and complete, to take you step by step towards your goals.

40%: Taking ACTION every single day.

Checkpoints

When I was at university, one of the subjects I participated in was orienteering. Basically, the lecturer would pre-determine a set course of checkpoints with special coordinates in the forest on particular trees. Individually, we would be required to use our compass to locate these throughout our journey, and you were judged on both speed and accuracy.

What this subject did teach me was the importance of careful planning, knowing my end destination and having visual checkpoints. For those of us participating, we didn't have any idea of what the middle part of the journey would look like, the challenges we would face between each checkpoint or the environmental conditions. What we did enjoy was the journey between point A (start) and Point Z (finish), and at times we were required to participate solo, while other times it was a team journey.

On reflection, the orientation subject is so much like starting your own business adventure, or establishing and moving towards your goals. You need to plan where you want to end up by developing checkpoints throughout the journey that confirm you are on the correct path. Enjoying the journey is a huge part because once you reach the end line, you will celebrate, pause and be ready for the next challenge!

The checkpoints in the design of your goals don't need to be hugely detailed, to begin with. They can be items that you need to complete in order to move from one task to the next towards your endpoint. As an example, let's assume that your goal is to develop an investment stock/share portfolio with an investment of $3,000.

To commence the planning phase, you need to get out a blank A4 piece of paper and brainstorm all the items that need to be completed. You then need to work through in order of priority of what needs to be completed from start to end.

The starting point (my goal) – I would like to develop a stock portfolio and invest $3,000 over 12 months.

The checkpoints below are made on the assumption that you would have some form of employment:

Checkpoint One – Determine the best way to gradually build my portfolio every month with a financial commitment.

Checkpoint Two – Arrange to have $250 every month automatically transferred from my pay on the 15th of every month, which is my payday.

Checkpoint Three – Set up the automatic transfer with my bank and establish a separate account. I will call this 'My Investing Portfolio Account.'

Checkpoint Four – Seek advice on the best platform to set up my online stock/share portfolio. Complete the required registration process and link up to my bank account.

Checkpoint Five – Seek financial counsel on the most appropriate stock/share that's suitable for your financial situation.

Side note: As a starting investor, it may be best to investigate a share that covers the top 200 businesses in your particular market, to diversify your risk rather than a standalone business in one industry.

Final Checkpoint – Once the stock is chosen, diarize for when the automatic transfers accumulate to $1,000, and this is when I will invest my money via the online platform. This will occur every four months.

By following the above checkpoints, I will have invested $3,000 over the 12-month period, and it only takes six key actions to ensure I achieve this goal. Importantly, try and automate the process, and you can then 'set and forget'. There is an excellent book called *The Automatic Millionaire* by David Bach that I would highly recommend on this topic.

As you can see, your destination map requires 'checkpoints' along the journey to ensure you are maintaining the right course. For the above scenario, it took me 15 minutes to work through the above steps that will allow me to achieve my desired goal. By doing this and having checkpoints in writing, you can physically tick them off as they're completed, and you can see your progression occurring. If you can't spare 15-20 minutes to develop your checkpoints, then don't be surprised if your goal is never realized. It's a simple yet very effective method.

Depending on the size of your goal, you may need to spend a number of hours, days or even weeks developing the initial blueprint of your destination checkpoints. As mentioned, if you are not willing to invest the time into the initial preparation, or don't have the commitment to fulfil the daily actions to achieve your goal, then it will be very challenging to have a clear view of what needs to be done. Visualization by itself isn't enough! It's all in the planning and taking action on the required steps.

Assignment Task

Step 1.

To start with, I would advise that you purchase an A4, 180-page binder book. Alternatively, there is a 'Goal Planning' template as the back of this book.

Step 2.

You need to write your goal down on the front page in BIG BOLD WRITING and place it on the bottom of the page with your goal in the past tense.

Step 3.

On the following pages, you then need to begin to develop the critical checklist of items or coordinates that you need to action and complete on your journey to achieve your goal. It may be worth using a scrap piece of paper initially to get all your coordinates down, before transferring this into a neat list with tick boxes – to mark when you complete each item – and a completion date.

Step 4.

Prioritize each step so all your focus and energy can go into that priority task before moving onto the next.

No Failures - Just Life Lessons

We are often paralyzed by the fear of failure. It's very easy to give up. You just have to say the words "I give up", and it's all done. Quite often, people go for the path of least resistance. The one that's the easiest. We are often trapped into not taking risks and living in our comfort zones because people develop the mentality that if they fail at a task, they fail as a person.

Do you take the stairs, or do you take the escalator? Do you eat the salad roll or choose the fries? Do you drive lap after lap, trying to secure a car park close to the shopping centre entry, when there are plenty 100 meters away that would take you 40 seconds to walk? These are often the initial indications of people that prefer the easy way. Is that you?

"We are often trapped into not taking risks and living in our comfort zones because people develop the mentality that if they fail at a task, they fail as a person."

As children, most of us learnt to ride a bike when we are four or five years old. We started on our training wheels, and once our parents felt we had enough experience and confidence, we'd graduate to just the two wheels.

However, all of us have experienced many falls from a bike in our younger years, but our resilience shone through. With tears in the eyes, stubbed toes grazed knees and hands; we were encouraged to get back on the bike many, many times over and to give it another go.

So, what changes from learning to ride a bike through to adulthood, when many give up challenges so quickly? I believe it's a combination of many factors that are either directly or indirectly imparted on us over the years.

We have no fear as children, and as our young brain begins to develop, the environment around us starts to apply the 'dream brakes' on what we think is possible. It might be through friends at school, brothers or sisters, social media, relatives or even complete strangers, but our confidence starts to get knocked around. We start to conform to what society expects of us rather than what we really want, and it's only the super determined, strong-willed or mighty confident kids that put all the noise to the side to stay on their true course to early success.

The single biggest barrier is yourself. The moment that you realize that you have control over your thoughts, reactions and feelings, the closer you will be to understanding that all fears are self-imposed. I certainly accept that there are real threats to your life; however, start to determine if other fears you encounter are real or perceived.

"I've missed more than 9,000 shots in my career. I've lost 300 games. 26 times I've been trusted to take the games winning shot and missed. I've failed over and over again in my life, and that's why I succeed."

Michael Jordan

Changing course

On my own personal journey, there have been countless times that my goals have changed from the initial plan, so just accept that it's part of your journey and move forward. There are goals that may appear to be right at the time, but circumstances do change.

Goals also have a tendency to change or adjust as you continue to re-evaluate your journey. Opportunities such as travelling abroad for work may have an impact, or perhaps a health concern, an inheritance, the death of a loved one, starting a family or even inspiration to start a new business can change your perspective on your goal setting. One day a goal may seem important to you, but the next, it may change, so there is a level of flexibility with the goal-setting process. What you should avoid is chopping and changing too often and just giving up because it is too hard. You certainly need to have conviction towards your goals, so should any challenges come your way, you are not just going to use that excuse to cast a goal astray because now it's in the 'too hard basket'. This is your opportunity to build resilience and keep on course to achieving your goal.

As you develop stronger habits, increase your confidence and begin to reduce your limiting beliefs, your thermostat for success and wealth will build. You should also use this as an opportunity to re-evaluate your goals to ensure they are in alignment with who you are now, not who you were before. What may have been a goal for you two years ago could well be set too low for where your journey has taken you to this point. Importantly, think of your goals as flags on different mountain tops. From your advantage point (your daily visualization), you can see all of the flags representing your goals as you turn 360 degrees. You can see them, you can't touch them, but they are there. With every mountain you climb, with every success you have and by building your skills and expertise, you become more experienced to handle the variety of environmental conditions that are going to come your way. The smaller mountains will become easy, but you will be ready to tackle the huge mountains as you climb towards your biggest goals.

Front of Mind

As mentioned in Chapter 1, goal setting has a very powerful partner in visualization and if used correctly, can significantly increase your ability to achieve your goals. The often-forgotten partner in this process – with equal superpowers – is 'The Daily Reminder'.

For the majority of people with a strong goal focus, they write down their goals and create a visual board. The goals may be reviewed weekly, and they stay relatively on target. This is great, but what I'm about to show you will take you to the next echelon and allow you to join the 'High Performers Club'.

Let me run through the three ways you can give it everything you have got!

The Daily Goal Review

I encourage you every day to spend just two minutes in the morning or two minutes in the afternoon (or both) to look over your goals, re-write your TOP 10 every day and read them out loud. If you can do both – the AM and PM – that's even better! This process will continue to re-enforce your goals in your subconscious.

Be Consistent

Write down your goals and place them in locations that you regularly visit. For example, my goals are placed on the wall in front of my work station; therefore, when I look up during the day, I have my vision board and goals directly in front of me at eye level. I also have them placed on the door of my wardrobe. Each time I go to get clothes out for the day, my goals are right in front of me. I've known of people that laminate their goals and place them on the shower screen door!

Journaling

Things really started to change for me when I developed my own 'Daily Goal Tracker'. It's my way of kick-starting the day, knowing what I want to achieve and building confidence in my abilities.

I implement the following structure:

AM
- I list 1-2 things that I'm grateful for.
- I list three things I will action throughout the day that will move me closer to my goals.
- I physically write down on a blank piece of paper my top 10 goals and read them out loud.
- Weekly, I rate myself out of 10 across the following key areas of Health, Self-Investment, Happiness and Wealth.

PM
- I list the things I achieved in the day.
- I note the minutes/hours that I exercised.
- I note one thing that I felt was really important or great about the day.
- I read over my goals.

The end of each week, I complete a self-audit and reflect back on what I have achieved and the momentum I have built. It's unbelievable what you can achieve in one week when you document it and structure your day and manage your time really efficiently. You begin to become conscious of every minute of the day and avoid unnecessary time-wasting activities such as surfing the web, checking your phone or non-productive discussions.

This is a section of the book that I really hope you pause and take ACTION on. Feel comfortable to take a break and do the following before moving forward. These are the moments that can change your life as you begin to recognize the importance of taking those actions that will move you to a new chapter or path in your life.

Assignment Task:

1. Write up three copies of your goals for either 12 months, three years or five years.
2. Place these goals in three prominent locations.
3. Create your own 'Daily Reflective Journal' or purchase one online.

MASTER SUCCESS PRINCIPLE #3

SUPPORTIVE HABITS

How to Develop Your Habits and Reach Your Goals?

To be different to the average person (the 90/10 rule), you need to develop habits that the top 10% are doing. Basically, you need to do more of the things that the average person isn't prepared to do! The average person might get up at 7.15 am for five days per week and sleep in on the weekends. The average person might buy take-away food twice per week, rather than making nutritious meals each night that are healthier for you. The average person might exercise twice per week and stop exercising when winter comes, rather than exercising 5-6 days per week all year round. The average person might watch two hours of TV per day, rather than reading a book for an hour. You get my drift!

"You need to do more of the things that the average person isn't prepared to do!"

An example of what your morning could look like, to be different from the average person:
Note: the below may not be suitable for all people and this is just an example of my routine.

4:25 AM - Wake up

4:30 AM - Power walk with my dog and listen to an educational podcast

5:05 AM - Drink 500 mL water and take one magnesium supplement

5:07 AM - Breakfast of porridge with fresh fruit and one scoop of natural yoghurt

5:16 AM - 120 push-ups (4 sets of 30)

5:20 AM - 200 sit-ups (4 sets of 50)

5:30 AM - Personal daily goal affirmations (recorded and played back)

5:35 AM - Meditation and visualization for 15 minutes

5:50 AM - The Daily Goal Tracker: Record what I'm grateful for, my current thoughts, and three key actions

6:00 AM - Shower

6:15 AM - Reading for 20 minutes

6:35 AM - Begin the day

*You should prepare and write down the tasks you need to do the night prior, so you get them out of your head and onto paper and this will allow your subconscious to start planning the day while you sleep.

"Motivation is what gets you started. Habit is what keeps you going."

Jim Rohn

To establish a supportive and robust habit, it needs to be continuous for about 60-90 days. This is the 'programming' aspect for the database entry for the brain. You will notice that things begin to automate themselves, like waking just before your alarm in the morning. It won't happen all the time, but you start to notice a significant shift in consciousness, and you can bounce out of bed so much easier.

To ensure you can establish and maintain a habit, you need to make things nice and easy and sustainable for yourself and develop a compelling reason to develop the habit. My BIG tip is not to make a significant change to your previous routine too quickly. For example, if you want to start waking up at 5.00 am, and you usually wake at 6.30 am, make incremental changes for a month by altering your alarm clock by 5-10 minutes every second day. Your body responds much better to change if it is incremental.

I'll give you an example of how to join the 5.00 am 'early up and go club' and what I did personally to establish my early morning routine.

Step One: I incrementally altered my alarm clock by five minutes each day over 30 days until my body was accustomed to rising at 5 am. I was still doing the below steps during the process, but this is how I joined the 5 am early risers' club (although a little earlier now!)

Step Two: I have my shoes, clothes, headphones and dog lead (I love to take my dog Ruby for my power walk) already in my home office before I go to bed, so I don't wake my wife when getting up in the morning. When you are half asleep, the last thing you want to be doing is searching around for socks and shoes at 5 am.

Step Three: I prepare my work clothes the night prior so again, I don't wake anyone else up in the household when getting ready for my 6.00 am shower.

Step Four: As I'm falling asleep every night, I visualize my end goal and tell myself that to achieve this goal, I need to rise at 5 am. It's the subconscious 'dream seed'.

Step Five: Set a peaceful sounding alarm. The last thing you want is to be startled by a sound resembling a car alarm!

Step Six: Catch yourself out if you hear that little voice saying "Just stay a little longer in bed. It's so cozy, and it's okay if you get up in five minutes".

Step Seven: Enjoy whatever you do for that first 30 minutes. Make it a good reason to get cracking. I have my favorite podcasts that I love to listen to, based on the interviews of successful people from across the globe. It's like having a 30-minute mentor and coaching session each morning. It sets the day up perfectly.

Don't assume that it is easy for me to rise early out of bed every morning with plenty of energy. There are mornings where I do struggle, but it is the clarity of my goals that helps me significantly. I have a big reason to rise and get going.

You may like to structure your morning routine very differently from mine, and that's perfectly fine. I appreciate that some of you would prefer to wait for the sun to rise before starting to walk the streets for your safety, or you may like to have your breakfast first and do some reading before starting your exercise. You may even want to incorporate a rest day (e.g. Sunday) that you can have a bit more of a sleep-in. My advice though is never to have two consecutive rest days as you will quickly lose the rhythm unless the reason is due to illness.

The importance of daily habits and structure

Let me start with a strong statement: without regular and consistent daily habits, you will fail to be able to take the required daily actions to achieve the success you aspire to.

To use a building analogy, you need to initially establish strong foundations that will enable the structure to be strong, be able to resist strong wind and rain, resist movements in the soil and take the weight of the building that stands upon it. The foundations are your daily habits, and without these, you might as well build your house with mud, in the sand and on the side of a hill. At some point, things will breakdown, the structure will fail, and your house will topple over.

"Without strong and consistent daily habits, you will fail to be able to take the required daily actions to achieve the success you aspire to."

I'll give you an example for some morning daily habits and why I use them personally.

Early Exercise

I wake at this time to get an early start to the day with my exercise and with far fewer distractions than I would if it were later in the morning. It's such a peaceful and relaxing part of the day. Remember, if you do more of the things that the average person isn't prepared to do, you know you are in front!

The other benefit of waking at early, is I get an extra two hours more than the average person of productive time to spend on my health and education. Over a five-day week, that's 10 hours extra, and over a month, it's 40 hours. That's one full extra working week in just that month alone! Extend that over 12 months, and it calculates to be 13 weeks or just over 3 months.

During the first 30 minutes of the day, I listen to a great motivational podcast with interviews by the great thinkers and high performers from across the globe. Over the week, I'm therefore listening to more than 2.5 hours of fantastic content, insights and educational information that can help my development and pass that onto others too.

Early Breakfast

An early breakfast gets the energy levels up and going and helps with your metabolism. Your breakfast needs to consist of things like fresh fruit (either cut up or in a smoothie); some yoghurt; a really large glass of water (500ml); perhaps some porridge that provides a slow-burning energy source; some green leafy vegetables, like spinach; or even some grilled tomatoes and avocado. Please avoid large 'heavy' breakfasts that contain meats like sausage, bacon, deep-fried hash browns or breakfasts with high-processed sugars.

Following breakfast, I'm ready for my next daily habit of visualization as part of my morning structure.

Visualization (15 - 20 mins)

I relax with my self-recorded ocean sound for 15 - 20 minutes, six days a week. I concentrate on my breathing for the first 1-2 minutes, and then I begin to visualize myself, achieving one of my BIG goals. In the initial few weeks, you may feel yourself drifting, but don't let that discourage you. Your preference may be to try traditional meditation, but mine is a hybrid model that works well for me. It took me 2-3 months to get into a solid rhythm, but now I look forward to this time every morning. This daily habit gets my brain tuned in and brings awareness for opportunities that could present throughout each day. Some of my most creative thinking and ideas have occurred during this time.

My 'Daily Goal Tracker' (5-10 mins)

Refer back to Success Principal #2 for an outline of my AM 'Daily Goal Tracker'. This document is my blueprint for the day and holds me accountable to the three key tasks or actions that I need to complete that day to move me closer to my goals. The tracker is also my barometer for how I feel I'm progressing and is an excellent reflection resource. During this time, I also re-write my Top 10 goals and re-read over my 12-month goals and those I've set for the day ahead. I then know ahead of time what my priorities for the day are and what time may need to be allocated to each task.

Reading – Self Improvement

Finally, it's essential to keep improving your skills and knowledge by reading. Just 30 minutes each morning equates to three hours a week minimum.

To start with, aim to read an average of one book each month. You will be amazed at what you learn with 12 books per year and what you can begin to implement into your own life. The average adult reads less that one non-fiction book per year so you will be strides ahead of anyone else. If you allocate 2 hours per day to personal education, you will be in the top 0.5% of people in the world!

Shower And Ready For The Day

For the final 10-15 minutes, I shower, change and get ready for the day. I'm well equipped to start with a massive amount of momentum after exercising, having a nutritious breakfast, reading, visualizing, scheduling my day, looking over my goals and listing the three key actions that I need to complete. You may choose different daily habits that are more suited to your lifestyle, but as long as you have them in place, that's the priority. But remember, it can take anywhere from 60-90 days to get into the rhythm of a habit, but that rhythm can be lost within days if it's not consistent, so don't let it slip for more than two days in a row.

Building Your Daily Habits Up Slowly

You can't expect to adopt a habit immediately, particularly significant impacting habits. As mentioned in the previous chapter, I simply didn't go from getting up at 7:00 am to suddenly decide that 5:00 am would be a more appropriate time to get more out of the day. In _Million Dollar Habits_ by Brian Tracy, he says, "_The fact is that good habits are hard to form but easy to live with. Bad habits, on the other hand, are easy to form but hard to live with. In either case, you develop either good or bad habits as a result of your repeated choices, decisions, and behaviors._"

You can build any strong habit with small incremental changes, and I strongly encourage you to introduce them with this method. It's like the way you would train for a 1km (0.6 miles) swim if you are not a swimmer. Every few days at swimming training, if you increased the distance by 25m (one lap in most pools) from a base start of 100m, then your capacity to build up your swimming fitness to cover the 1km would be between 10-12 weeks depending on your training frequency.

Along similar lines to building towards specific times for your daily habits, it's also advisable to slowly include new habits into your structure too. Many make the mistake of trying to introduce five-morning habits immediately. When this occurs, they feel like they're jumping from one thing to another and rushing. Again, slow incremental changes are essential, and it would be sensible to introduce one new habit per week over five weeks. You then have the opportunity to test and trial the habits, and the time you'd like to allocate to each one. You may feel that 30 minutes of reading is too much, and perhaps 20 minutes will suffice. Keep trialing until you get the right mix and blend that's suitable to you and your goals.

Developing strong daily habits, particularly substantial changes to what you are used to, need to be built over an extended period. Don't try and be a superhero and attempt to leap over tall buildings from day one. Instead, learn to jump the puddle first and build up slowly. A daily habit has a more significant impact if it's recorded and remains a constant reminder. You need to become accountable for your actions and physically recording your habit ensures you stay consistent, to build the habit over a couple of months. It needs to be listed almost like a running sheet; listing the times and actions you need to complete, and the times they need to start and end by.

I'm regularly told that daily habits are challenging to maintain due to a variety of circumstances or even excuses. You need to treat your daily habits like you have enlisted in the army. The army is recognized for its strict policy on structure, and there are significant consequences for not abiding by the rules. The structure ensures that tasks need to be completed with precision, on time and with pride. This should be the same attitude that people need to adopt with their daily habits and treat them seriously. Start developing a dependency on them and become addicted to the amazing results they will help you achieve; the better the structure, the greater the chance that the habit will become ingrained into a regular routine and become automatic.

An important side note that I must reinforce when it comes to daily habits: what most high performers assume when talking about building in a structure for daily habits, is that people know what a 'good' habit is. A good habit, for your reference, is one that will continue to build a 'better version' of yourself. This may include improving your knowledge and education, your fitness, your health (physical and mental) and your wealth. Introducing bad habits will be detrimental to your growth and the opportunity to achieve your goals.

To build your daily habits and to set yourself apart from others, you must introduce habits that would usually be beyond the comfort zone of others. A daily habit structure like the below IS NOT what successful people do, although some people might think that because they have a structure, this will lead them to success. Does this look familiar to you?

7:00 am > Wake

7:15 am > Shower

7:30 am > Breakfast

8:00 am > Leave for work (listen to AM breakfast radio and news)

8:30 am-5:00 pm > Work

5:30 pm > Home and cook dinner

6:30 pm-10:00 pm > Watch TV

10:15 pm > Bed

REPEAT x five days!

Some may even include the occasional gym session, but to set yourself apart, you need to build 'game changers' into your daily habits that help you grow as a person.

Reflection

Reflecting *briefly* on where you have been and what you have achieved is an excellent way to build confidence for your journey ahead. The late Steve Jobs was quoted as saying *"You can't connect the dots looking forward; you can only connect them looking backwards, so you have to trust that the dots will somehow connect in your future. You have to trust in something be that your destiny, life, karma, whatever. This has never let me down, and it's been the difference in my life."*

In summary, things will happen to you on your journey, and you will wonder why it happened. It could be the break-up of a relationship; a job interview you missed out on or a business that didn't work out. What didn't go to plan can turn out to be a watershed moment that will throw you in a whole new direction. I often think back on a few job interviews that I missed out on. At the time, I was disappointed and couldn't work out why I missed out. I thought I interviewed well and would have been a great asset to the organization. On reflection, my life would have taken a very different turn. I may never have met my amazing wife if I'd moved to a different location, and therefore, we would never have had our two beautiful children. I may never have built up the experiences and skills from the corporate world to start my own business and could have remained as a school teacher in a small town for half my career. You can't be so attached to how life is supposed to work out, but rather, as Steve Jobs said, have trust that the dots of your journey will all be connected in the future.

It is essential to take the time at the end of each week – and at the end of each month – to conduct a self-audit on your progress. This will serve two purposes:

It demonstrates your action-orientated mentality and builds confidence, as you see forward momentum towards your goals; and

It ensures you take the time to enjoy your journey towards your goals. Don't be in such a rush that you forget to take in the scenery around you.

A great way of being able to maintain a record of your progress is to keep a daily journal, but not a typical journal that we're used to. Part of the 'Daily Goal Tracker' that I designed is to complete my self-audit on the seventh day (mine is a Sunday) and review what I've achieved. The weekly audit builds confidence to see how many things I accomplished, plus it establishes a new checklist of the things I want to achieve for the coming seven days.

On the seventh day, I spend 20 minutes reviewing the current week, but also carefully plan the week ahead. It helps me maintain rhythm, momentum and consistency in how I perform and keeps me accountable for what I want to achieve. The most significant review is conducted every four weeks, and you need to spend 30-45 minutes to evaluate the forward momentum you have achieved over the month or 30 days. The questions I ask myself are:

- What areas have I excelled in?
- What areas can I improve?
- What would I have done differently if I had my time over?
- Are their skills that I've learnt over the past four weeks?
- What have been some of my most significant achievements?
- Am I on track with the amount of exercise I've completed?
- Is there anything that has limited my growth and momentum?

As well as developing a forward mentality with your goals and visualization, reflecting on what you have needed to action to get you to this stage is highly important. Your daily, weekly and monthly reflective journal will also be a fantastic resource that you and others can draw from, to gain knowledge and experience in the years to come. At times, it feels like a surreal experience when I reflect back on my journal, as I'm blown away with how much I've achieved; and I guarantee, you will too with your own journal!

Procrastination and Fear of Failure

For many, starting something new can be challenging, mainly if it involves extended periods of motivation and commitment. As mentioned earlier, procrastination can be a handbrake to achieving your goals. The fear can develop from a perceived 'end result' that's not favorable; therefore, they freeze and can't progress forward. Whatever the reason, procrastination can indeed hold you back. Some people's fears grow, and they start to build on the story to justify their fear. Studies have shown that 50% of the stories we make up about our fears are not actually even accurate, and 90% won't even eventualize.

Research has proven that when people are on their 'death bed', they don't regret the things they did, rather the things they didn't do. Imagine the things you would try if you knew that failure wasn't a possibility: starting that business, investing in the share market, purchasing an investment property, authoring your own book, learning to play the guitar, starting a family or travelling to a dream location.

'Fear of Failure' can paralyze the most hardened individual in a variety of circumstances. For many, they feel that failure will be looked upon negatively by others, and our position in society will be lessened. The only time you will be judged harshly by failure is if you have acted without integrity, have been disloyal or have been deceitful. If you have tried and failed, you have nothing at all to be ashamed of. You should be proud that you have taken that huge leap of faith. As Thomas Edison once said, "*I have not failed, I've just found 10,000 ways that won't work.*"

Failure is just another way of finding out that you need to try something a different way and move out of your comfort zone. It doesn't mean that it was necessarily wrong. It may have been your timing, external influences that were out of your control, or even the order of your execution. Too many people don't realize that they are so close to getting it right, but instead, choose to give up rather than change perhaps the one % to make it right. Strength of mind and resilience are learned through failure, and some of the most significant and most important accomplishments in the world would never have proceeded past the testing stage if it hadn't been for those individuals with incredible resilience and a mindset to conquer their fears. Make it your life's commitment to 'never ever give up'.

What Can Cure Procrastination?

Curing procrastination is like rebooting your computer for an update of the software. For a significant change, it will take time, particularly if you have been delaying the inevitable for months and months or even years. On the other hand, if you are open to change, it can take no time at all! Like most things, the bigger the change, the bigger the effort, the longer the timeline. It can also be dependent on your resistance to change, your motivation to make it happen, and the goals you have.

As young children, we are open to programming from a variety of different people and experiences. Many of our limiting beliefs and fears are the result of what was programmed into our brain at a young age. We do an incredible amount of observation when we're young, but over time, it becomes harder to reprogram our thought patterns and behaviors as adults.

You can have all the 'intention' to change, but without taking action, you will continue to walk a similar, well-worn path for years until you say "enough is enough". You need to stop the conversation when you hear yourself saying "my intention is to do this" or "I had the intention to do that". Rather, you should be saying "I am going to do this by the 10th September" or "I will start that today". You need to make a conscious effort to use action-oriented language that alters your thinking patterns, as it reinforces a commitment to get it done and with a timeline. Try it from now on, and you will be pleasantly surprised at how much something so simple can impact your life so significantly.

To break the habit of procrastination, introduce just

one single daily action that will help you to kick start the process. Let's call it a 'micro-action'. As the name suggests, the action is small but helps with your reprogramming. With each daily 'micro-action', you begin to gain confidence as you start to get items 'ticked off'. The momentum of this action builds day by day and compounds over time. Just say you did one single 'micro-action' seven days a week; this would accumulate to 365 a year. Imagine the separation you'd create between your current self and your new self by completing 365 additional actions! At some point, you might be comfortable to build that up to two a day. It's those small introductions into your daily life that compound and make a huge difference over one year, three years or even five years.

MASTER SUCCESS PRINCIPLE #4

TAKE CONTROL

When to Expect Success?

When you combine careful planning, repeated daily actions, a robust structure and a commitment to your goal, then you will be in the top 10 % of achievers. What is often forgotten in this formula is 'patience'. If you set out to move closer to your goals every day, then your tolerance will build for any challenges you face. You see, by moving closer to your goals, you build confidence and happiness in your day and any frustration will dissipate if you can physically 'tick off' the actions you complete.

"Two things define you: your patience when you have nothing and your attitude when you have everything." Anon

A great way to think of this would be to implement the 'Action Compounder'. The more actions that you implement, the more they build over time and the more goals you can achieve. I've repeated this several times throughout this book, but the compounding effect that doing daily actions can have on your life is enormous. If you were to just complete two micro-actions each day over 3 years, you would have completed 2,190 actions!

Celebration

Don't be so quick to jump to your next goal once you have achieved one as there needs to be a kind of 'circuit breaker' that allows you to enjoy the moment and soak in what you have achieved. It doesn't need to be a huge party, an expensive restaurant or involve fireworks. It could be your favorite meal at the local hotel, a barbecue with family and friends or even a movie with your partner or sibling. It just needs to be an occasion that is special to you and an opportunity to reflect on your achievement. By having these celebrations, it provides an incentive in your subconscious; we're attracted to joy, happiness, laughter and fun, and your motivation will continue to be strong if you stop and celebrate. As they say, take the time to stop and smell the roses.

Little wins and small celebrations should never be lost throughout your journey. One key thing is to not only celebrate your own wins but the achievements of others. As we all know, it's such a nice feeling when people recognize the commitment and effort that you have made to achieve a special goal. You can be humble on the outside if you choose, but make sure you are screaming inside with excitement when they congratulate you! Perhaps it's only with your closest friends or family that you can literally jump for joy. Congratulating others needs to be done with sincerity, and they will feel your energy and excitement. Don't get so caught up in your own world that you forget about those that are also striving to be their best and reach the summit of their mountain.

MASTER SUCCESS PRINCIPLE #5

GOAL OBSESSION

Your Capacity to Push On.

What would you be prepared to sacrifice to achieve your goals? Rising at 5:00 am rather than 7:00 am, working on a Friday night or spending that time in front of the TV? Purchasing a second-hand car with 80,000kms on the odometer, or buying a brand-new car to impress people you don't care about and will put you into debt?

If you develop the right goals and they are really what you want, then there shouldn't be any questioning on your ability to succeed. It is only when you develop goals with the 'I wish' attitude, or when you are not prepared to sacrifice things in your life, that your dreams start to evaporate. Even worse, having someone else design the goals for you! Remember, you want to fulfil *your* goals, not theirs.

As a short side note to sacrificing things, there may be non-negotiables that you need to consider. For example, you need to be considerate of your relationships with family or friends. Yes, you may need to commit more time in the mornings, nights and weekends to move closer towards your goals, but what's the point in life if you achieve your goals, but you have nobody to celebrate the achievements with

Working out the level of effort and sacrifice required to achieve a BIG goal isn't always evident from the very beginning, but it will soon dawn upon you that at some level, all goals require commitment and a level of sacrifice. It may be as small as putting aside $3 a day towards a financial goal, getting out of bed an hour earlier in the morning, giving up your daily coffee or walking to work rather than driving. The length of time you allocate for a goal to be achieved will also dictate the level of sacrifice required. If your goal was to author a 30,000-word book over a one-year period rather than two years, then you are going to need to invest twice as much time in a shorter period. It may require 5.00 am starts rather than 6.30 am, or writing six evenings a week rather than three or four. Only *you* can determine how quickly you'd like to achieve a goal and what price you are willing to pay. The question is, are you prepared to double your motivation and commitment to get what you want?

Shared goals with your partner, family, friends, work colleagues or teammates can also be very powerful, as you have a common goal to achieve.

You can be there for each other to encourage, support and motivate each other to achieve your particular goal. Shared goals can work particularly well when it's quite substantial, like purchasing a home, starting a business, planning an overseas holiday or planning to win a grand-final. There are times that your drive and commitment may wane, however, if you have got someone else or a group of individuals aligned and accountable for your goal, you can really help each other out. There's also something very, very special about achieving a shared goal with a group of people or someone you care deeply for.

Your Commitment

We have all been enthusiastic about something at some point in our lives. Perhaps it's going for a run with the intention of improving our fitness, or perhaps it's organizing a party or attending a major event. Whatever the reason, if you are not 'committed' to the end result, then your initial enthusiasm will diminish and eventually die off. Think of enthusiasm as the adrenalin injection you get when something exciting has occurred; you feel instant euphoria and drive to make it happen. Over time, the initial excitement from the adrenalin passes and your initial 'bounce' will flatten out. Enthusiasm though is the initial key ingredient to setting your goals and helps develop that core belief and commitment for the long term. Always embrace enthusiasm, but bring it together with your strong commitment to the task.

> **"In winners, commitment is what remains behind after enthusiasm has died in others."**
> Robin Sieger

The 10 Key Pillars of a Healthy Mindset

There are 10 key pillars that I believe will give you every opportunity to maintain a healthy mindset and all must flow from each other. I never like to complicate things, and my aim here is to lay them out so that they can be implemented easily into your life. I believe they allow you to form a healthy mindset, as they complement each other and in combination, they will *turbo-boost* your momentum towards success and fulfilment, therefore leading to a healthy mindset.

<u>One</u>
Set Your Goals

Goal setting opens you up a whole world of opportunities that you may not be aware of. By developing your clear goals, it gives you clarity on your 'WHY', and this will enable you to set yourself up perfectly to carry out the next nine pillars.

<u>Two</u>
A Healthy Diet, Daily Exercise and The Right Amount of Sleep

Your diet, health and sleeping patterns dictate your capacity to function to your full capacity on a daily basis. A change in any of these three key areas has an impact as they're all interlinked. Your diet forms the fuel for your body, your exercise builds strength across your body (heart, lungs, muscles, brain, et cetera), and your sleep allows your body to rejuvenate and repair.

Maintaining your health is so important, and without good health, you will never be able to enjoy the great things you have worked so hard to achieve. My point? Keep it all in balance and ensure you take really good care of your health and fitness because, without it, you won't be around long enough to enjoy the fruits of your labor.

THREE
Good Daily Habits

Your daily habits form the foundation and structure to set up your day and maintain good practices, for building success and achieving your goals. Examples of daily habits may include:

Between 25-30 minutes of daily exercise

20-minutes meditation or visualization exercise

Eating a healthy and nutritious breakfast

Maintaining a daily journal and recording one or two things you are grateful for

Writing down your top 10 goals and your top three priorities or actions for the day and numbering off all other tasks in order of priority at the conclusion of each day, recording the tasks and priorities for the next day.

FOUR
Gratitude

Displaying gratitude has been proven to boost your fulfilment in life. Each day, you need to write down one or two things that you are grateful for in your life. It can be a reflection of your past, current-day events, travel experiences, family and friends, successes you have achieved or opportunities you have received. Gratitude provides balance in our life.

By achieve the right balance; the daily gratification process allows you to reflect on what amazing things you already have but also charges you with the opportunity to strive for more. If you think you have everything, then you will shy away from developing and striving each and every day towards achieving your goals. Gratification positions us in a place where we feel open to receive, and this is as important as giving.

FIVE

Love and Appreciate Your Friends, Family and Your Community

There are things you can live without, but not love. To be able to love and be loved is a human feeling that we crave. You can have a billion dollars in the bank, but you'd feel '*worthless*' without the love of your close friends and family. Money and materialistic items can be won, purchased or even earned in an instant, but not love.

You see many people that sacrifice friendships and family on their way to scale the mountain to financial wealth, but when they get to the top and look over their shoulder, there's nobody there. They realise that the view from the top is very lonely without someone you love to share it with. At the end of your life, you will reflect on the relationships you have forged, the people you have met, the places you have visited, your family holidays, shared laughter and the positive impact you have had on other people, and not the money sitting in your bank.

SIX
It's Not What You Are Dealt with in Life; It's How You Deal with It

In life, we're thrown plenty of challenges to navigate, and we all react to them differently. Some people are calm; others freak out and curl up into the fetal position. Others might be calm, to begin with, but they overthink and dissect things, getting themselves, all twisted up and unable to think straight. Whatever challenge, incident, or event you are thrown, you have the choice about how you respond. Your response may be based on previous events, perhaps from your childhood or even how your parents may have responded, and you are mirroring their reactions. The best leaders in the world respond calmly and methodically to pressure situations. They lead from the front and keep their team calm. They take in all the information, assess the situation and make a decision based on their experience that will be in the best interests of those individuals they lead. Can you imagine our world if the most powerful leaders – and those with the biggest responsibilities – reacted with panic and haste every time on events that they were involved in! It does occasionally happen and usually with a significant impact on millions of people.

Ultimately, we are in complete control of our emotions and the way we respond to events. It's so true that things happen *for* us and not *to* us. We need to listen to what challenges the universe is testing us with, as they are all learning opportunities. It may not appear like that at the time but reflect back on some of the challenges you have experienced in life so far, and understand the lessons and the direction you have taken in your life because of those events.

SEVEN
Positively Impact Others

In life, I believe we all get the opportunity to positively impact others. It may be as a teacher, a volunteer, a parent, a brother, a sister, an uncle, an aunty, a manager and in many, many other ways. To gift someone with positive influence comes in many various forms, and the impact may be for just one person or millions of people.

Some feel they don't have anything to teach or to give that will have a positive impact, but it can be just the small things: helping a mother with her pram up some stairs; opening the door for someone to let them through, or even offering up your seat on a busy train to an elderly person. These are all small things you could be doing to positively impact someone's day. If you help someone out this way, they're likely to return the favor to another person in a similar situation.

"You can get everything in life you want if you will just help enough other people to get what they want."
Zig Ziglar

EIGHT
Be Kind to Others

Any decent and respectful human being should live by the following two values:

- *Treat EVERYBODY with respect, kindness and love; and*
- *Treat people like you would like to be treated yourself.*

Next time you are out with a new acquaintance, a friend or work colleague, listen and watch out for the way they treat others in a restaurant, café or a shop. It's a very quick indicator of how they respect all people no matter what religion, race, job or social status they have.

How you treat others is a direct reflection of YOU. You may claim to be a 'quality person' and someone with high values but think carefully of the way you treat and respect others. Do you demonstrate integrity? Are you polite? Do you follow up and deliver on your promises? And would you come to the aid of a stranger that needs help? There are many situations where you can be kind to others, even if these people aren't kind to you.

NINE

Invest in Yourself and Your Wealth

Jim Rohan has a wonderful quote of *"work harder on yourself than you do at your job".* Simply put, the investments that you make in yourself will significantly increase your value through your knowledge and applications you can use with your experiences. You must commit to investing the time to learn these skills and use a wide variety of resources to obtain them.

These days, you can tap into the minds of many of the most successful people on the planet by listening to interviews on podcasts, watching online videos, reading their books or attending seminars and workshops. If you go back to even the late 1990s, there was limited accessibility for the average person on the street to listen and learn from these people, without having to pay thousands of dollars to attend live events or purchase the old DVD sets. These days you can view them on YouTube for free.

A little while ago, I made that conscious decision to stop listening to music in the car and the usual morning breakfast radio as I commuted for work.

From that single decision, I now listen to an average of eight hours per week of amazing podcasts that broaden my knowledge. Over the month, this equates to 32 hours of education and knowledge, rather than negative news stories and repetitive music. Over a period of 2 years, the equivalent of some university degrees!

Books are also an amazing way to gain knowledge. For the price of $20-$30, where else can you go to learn the stories, lessons, knowledge and experiences from a person without having the opportunity to sit with them personally? I'm a traditional kind of person and love being able to read books in hard copy rather than online. It's also quite exciting to receive a new book in the mail. It's like opening my own special birthday gift! I'll re-read my favorite books many times over, highlighting sections, placing sticky notes in the pages and taking them on holidays to relax. I think that e-books do have a place, but it may only suit a proportion of the population that is happy to read off their screens.

TEN

Make Each Day Count

Did you know that if you are 30 years old and the average life expectancy is 85, you only have around 660 months remaining on earth? For many, they feel that 'old age' is in the far distant future, and they continue to cruise through life. I distinctly remember my mum's 40th birthday when I was in my early teens and it's so hard to fathom where those past 30 years have gone.

I'm not sure if it's due to us being connected 24/7 to technology or not, but time feels like its passing by faster and faster each year. Weeks go by in a flash, and the months feel like they've been reduced to 20 days. The only thing that all of us *can't* have more of is time. There are 24 hours in a day, and that's it! What you do with your 1440 minutes will define who you are, the success that you generate and the experiences you have. I made a conscious decision to make more use of my time and rather than going to bed at 10 pm and waking at 6.30 am; I'd go to bed at 9.30 pm and wake at 4.30 am. Traditionally, the hours of 8-10 pm are used up by watching TV, so I decided that once I'd had some nice family time with my wife and my kids and they headed off to bed at 8.30 pm, I would read for an hour and then go to bed at 9.30 pm. I then rise at 4.30 am, giving me an additional two hours each morning to 'invest' in myself. Those extra two hours in the morning add up to 10 hours a week, or 40 hours a month (based on five days). A total of 40 hours over 12 months equals 480 hours – or an extra 13 working weeks (based on the average 40hr work week) of self-investment each year. If you started this at the age of 40 and continued to the age of 65, you would have invested an additional 75 months or 6.25 years.

By using this simple technique, you could add years to your physical and mental wellbeing along with the extraordinary knowledge you would gain in life by altering your daily habits and behaviors. All it takes is some discipline, commitment and a goal to want to do more, be more and achieve more. Again, it's another investment that you can make in yourself that will not just help with your mental health and knowledge, but help others with the knowledge you can share.

MASTER SUCCESS

PRINCIPLE #6

OVERCOME FEAR
OF FAILURE

Keep Pushing

The thermometer of fear is very different in each of us. What is feared by one person is happily accommodated by someone else. Fear can be introduced at any stage of our life, but our limiting beliefs are usually a direct result of something that has occurred to us in childhood. Those limiting beliefs are generally fear-related and can stop us from achieving the success we crave.

Fear can also increase with age and responsibility. A 38-year-old is less likely to start their own business if they have a mortgage, children and school fees to pay through the *fear* that they might 'lose it all' if the business doesn't work out. Fear is also a great 'excuse' generator and creates procrastination to creep into your mindset. If someone makes an excuse about not wanting to do something, you will generally find some kind of fear beneath the layers that have caused this inaction. If you do have a particular fear, try and isolate that fear and mitigate its influence and just take the first step.

For example, if your fear is that you won't be able to start your own business because you can't pay the rent or weekly food and utility bills, then consider one of the below ideas:

Automate a percentage of your pay to go directly into a separate bank account that will cover your living expenses for a period of four months prior to making the leap of faith. It may take you 12 months or longer to accumulate, but once you have that amount accrued, you then have comfort that you can tap into that account if you need to.

Don't just commence your own business without seeking out some casual or part-time work to bring in enough money to contribute towards your mortgage, rent, utilities and food, even if it's some night-shift work. Your employer may be open for you to work an eight-day fortnight. That way, you have one day a week that you can immerse yourself in developing some momentum to start your business. Remember, at the end of the day, you still have your experience and resume but remain strong and tell yourself that you are never ever going to give up.

You may never be able to fully mitigate your fear, so be ready for that feeling that builds up inside of you. It's like a nervous, tingly feeling that makes your heart pump and distorts your clear-thinking capacity. If you think of your fear as a wall, you need to choose how you are going to conquer it. I don't care if the 'wall of fear' is conquered by running through it, around it or jumping over it, I just want you to choose one of them. To start the process, try and identify the root cause and then answer these questions:

- Is there potential for your fear to cause you physical harm if you try and overcome it?
- Is it a 'perceived' fear of what will happen, rather than what will most likely not even happen?
- Does everyone else share your fear? If not, why not?
- Is there someone that doesn't share your fear? If so, have you talked about their reason as to why they don't share that same fear, or how they think about the fear?
- What's the absolute worst thing that could happen if your fear was to become a reality? Are you making the fear bigger than what it really is?

If you could overcome your fear, what success could you achieve? Is the fear that great, that you would rather continue carrying that fear than overcome it and achieve the success you have always wanted?

Turn it on its head and ask 'what are the consequences or opportunities I'll miss if I don't try it?'

If you answer these questions honestly, it will help you to identify the perceived fear, what you need to do to overcome it, and the limitations it's causing for your future success.

That Little Voice That Says "NO."

Consciously or subconsciously, we are talking to ourselves all the time. It's not always through a little voice you sometimes hear, but by pure thought alone. People like to explain this phenomenon by using the 'angel and the devil on the shoulder' explanation. You have all seen it on cartoons before. The angel will be on the left shoulder, whispering the positive thoughts, while the devil on the right shoulder will be whispering to do the opposite. There's often quite the tug-of-war between the two to make a decision.

I didn't realise how much of an impact my inner voice was limiting my ability to turbo-boost my success. It was always trying to bring me back to my comfort zone rather than encouraging me to take bigger risks and move to the next level. It was like my mind had its own unique thermostat to return me back to neutral, rather than allowing me to push for greater things. The voice was even evident and sometimes still is, when I was developing my early morning habits of a 4.25 am wake-up: "Just stay in this cozy bed for another five minutes, there'll be no harm done." It's like there's a constant negotiation taking place between me and this other part of my brain.

You need to be very conscious of your inner voice and the more conscious you become of the little whispers and commentary, the more you will start to realise how much it's been holding you back. You see, inner voice has been completely responsible for establishing and forever bringing to your attention the fears that you have. This voice believes it's his or her responsibility to keep you safe from harm, even if there's no chance of you actually being hurt at all!

As you develop the awareness of inner voice and the ongoing negotiation between the two of you, you begin to become acutely aware and have the confidence to push back hard. Rather than hearing *no*, you flip it on its head and hear the word *GO*!

Over the next week, become conscious of the self-talk that's going on inside you. Take note of how often the voice is trying to turn back the 'progression' dial and limit your growth through limiting self-talk. There may only be a few small things you actually need to change in your thought process and decision-making that could make an enormous impact on your growth. Is the voice really 'protecting you', or simply 'limiting you' on where you are now compared to where you should be?

John Fitzgerald, one of Australia's most successful property investors, advises his clients that to grow a business, you need to do two things every day that you fear or don't like to do. With time, perseverance and plenty of mental strength, you become great at the things you *don't like* to do, and they're no longer a weakness. For example, if you had a fear of cold-calls to generate new sales leads, you'd make two cold-calls per day and overcome the fear. Two calls a day over the working week will be 10 per week, or 40 a month, and this could be the difference between an average business and a great business! Some leading sales consultants recommend making a minimum of 50 calls as quickly as possible with no pressure on making a sale to flush out the fear factor.

You choose – genuine or authentic?

Self-confidence is an energy form that can both help and hinder our ability to grow personally and professionally. Self-confidence can ooze from the pores of some people, but what appears on the surface may in fact be a cover for what they feel like deep down.

Self-confidence can only be 'faked' for a limited time before the true self starts to shine through. This is why being true to yourself and genuine to everyone around you is so important. Nobody likes to be 'conned', and there's something very off-putting about a person that's not authentic. In the long-term, the only person you will be fooling is yourself! It's all about being truthful, honest, having integrity and delivering on your promises. What I don't like are people who publicly state that they are 'genuine' or 'authentic' and are self-promoters. Don't self-proclaim because if it's true, others will be happy to sing from the rooftops and make that statement on your behalf. They're not words you have to say; they are things you need to be!

MASTER SUCCESS PRINCIPLE #7

PEOPLE POWER

Circle of Trust

Developing your own circle of trust is really important so you can seek out those that have either already achieved what you want or align yourself with like-minded people. There's no value in trying to 'guess' what to do next if it's already been done before. You will not only save valuable time and money, but you have probably got every opportunity to even make it better than the original. If you are honest, sincere, have a great attitude and are willing to learn, you will find that 99% of all people will be very open to helping you in a variety of forms. That may come in the way of a face-to-face catch-up, a conversation over the phone, an email or even a social media exchange. It will vary depending on your connection with that person and if you know them via your family, a friend, work connection or even if it's unsolicited. In a nutshell, just put yourself out there and ask.

By developing connections and even friendships with high-level achievers, you will start to get an understanding of what it takes to get to their level. To do this, you must ask quality questions. Great questions will draw out great answers, and that's where you will be able to grow yourself.

When considering who to include in your circle of trust, please consider these people very carefully. They must meet four specific criteria that I will outline below. Consider this process like you are shortlisting potential candidates to join your team of professional advisors to guide you in your personal business, to achieve the goals you want.

Qualities:

They are great people. They demonstrate great human qualities. These may include being friendly, open, honest, sincere, treating everyone with respect, leading by example, being generous, engaging in a healthy lifestyle, holding healthy relationships with others, or being positive and displaying habits that elevate them to the top 10 per cent. I wouldn't advocate for you to meet with people that have only made lots of money but don't share the above qualities.

Open to share. Provide you with honest answers regarding things that have worked well for them, along with failures that have made them stronger.

Have achieved things that you would like to achieve. Single out people that have achieved particular goals that you would like to achieve. Because we all strive to achieve different goals, no one person will have every goal you want to achieve, but they may have achieved one or a few of the goals that you aspire to.

Make you inspired. Members 'employed' in your circle of trust must have the qualities to inspire you. Please avoid at all costs those individuals that have the 'glass half full' mentality. These people fall into the 90 % rule. We're aiming for the top 10 % of achievers.

So, where do you find these people? Well, it starts with your notepad, so please grab it now before moving onto the action task below.

Assignment Action Task.

I want you to follow the next five steps:

Step One:
Write down any friends or family that you know that meet the four criteria points for shortlisting. Do they demonstrate a great work ethic and are achieving things that you would like to achieve in the next ten years? If it's only one person, that's

okay. If you can't isolate anyone that fits the criterion, move to Step 2.

Step Two:

Write down any current connections or business people that fall out of your initial family and friends circle. This may include business owners, former educators, managers, high-level sports coaches or players. Don't just think in the age bracket of 30-60 years. I have two mentors with one in his '70s and the other in his '80s who are incredibly insightful and provides me with so much knowledge.

Step Three:

Initially shortlist 3-4 candidates. You can always open up to connecting with more at a later date.

Step Four:

Reach out to these people. Depending on your existing relationship, this may be via a call, email or even a text message. Request an opportunity to meet for a coffee or lunch.

Rules:
- Be prompt with any responses to coordinate the catch-up.
- Offer a location that is convenient for them.
- Confirm the meeting the day prior.
- Take your notepad and make sure you note specific questions you want to ask before the meeting.
- Arrive five minutes prior to the catch-up.
- Be respectful to your catch-up meeting length and don't overstay your welcome.
- Take lots of notes.
- Cover the full bill.

Step Five:
On the same day, send the person a 'thank you' message via text or email to convey your appreciation for the opportunity to meet.

*"**Quality questions create a quality life. Successful people ask better questions, and as a result, they get better answers.**"*
Tony Robbins

Questions during your shortlisting process

It's important to think of the WHY prior to meeting with a mentor or leader. The first question is to yourself. Why am I meeting with this person? What knowledge am I seeking? This will then direct you to the questions you need to ask.

Some examples may be:

- What are your daily habits and rituals that you implement?
- How do you structure your day?
- To date, what has been life's biggest lessons?
- If you could rewind the clock, what would you have done differently?
- Who has been your biggest influence, and how have they helped you?
- What books would you recommend I read that have had an impact on you?
- If you had 60 seconds with me and needed to give me a life lesson, what would you say?
- Is there anybody you know that I could meet that could also help me with my journey?

Leadership & Influence

Do you influence a group of people, or simply just one person? Leadership isn't just isolated to business owners, coaches, captains, church leaders, PRINCIPLEs, teachers, parents or CEOs. Leadership falls with anyone that has influence over another individual. There are those that embrace leadership, while there are others that fear the responsibility. A great quote from John. C. Maxwell on leadership is *"A leader is one who knows the way, goes the way, and shows the way."*

Leadership is different from management. The ultimate compliment for a leader is to empower those in their team to become even better leaders in their own right. The manager, on the other hand, works from an instructional position and tells those in their team 'what to do', rather than empower them to make their own decisions.

There have been thousands of books written on leadership, each with their own 'angle' on how great leaders lead. The common thread amongst all the books is the opportunity to influence others, and this can be positive or negative. There have been leaders throughout history that have had a significant influence over others but have used their power for evil, causing significant injury, harm and death. There are also those that have had an incredible influence that has made the world a much better and more peaceful place; leaders like the Dalai Lama, Mother Teresa and Martin Luther King to name a few from the 20th century.

We all have the opportunity to influence and lead by example. There's no prerequisite for a strong and positive leader to have the ability to get up on stage or to be in charge of a large team. A strong leader and a person of influence should be prepared to be courageous, make the tough decisions even if they're not popular, be the first to accept criticism but also the first to share the credit with their team. They should not be focused on individual accolades but focused on the success of the team. Great leaders go shoulder-to-shoulder with their team when in battle and never leave anyone behind. They earn the respect of others, but never demand it and empower their team to be their very best version of themselves.

When given the opportunity, you should embrace leadership and the opportunity to positively impact those that you influence. Go on, take a look over your shoulder and make an impact for those that are behind you!

MASTER SUCCESS PRINCIPLE #8

OUR CHOICES

Choices

Throughout this book, you will notice that 'it's up to you' to make the decisions that will allow you to achieve your goals. When you are a child, many decisions are made on your behalf with most in relation to your safety and health. Your brain is still developing, and your ability to cognitively process some decisions may not necessarily be what is best for your health and safety.

As you enter adulthood, you enter a phase in your life where the majority of decisions you are making, start having a direct impact on the life you want to lead. That may come in the way of relationships with friends and family, the purchase of your first car, travel, religion, health and fitness, education, food choices, alcohol or drug consumption, and employment. It's important to start establishing the goals you want to achieve early, so you have every opportunity to set the best structures in place to help guide decisions in these focus areas. My position in this book isn't to lecture you about the decisions you need to be making in these areas, but to highlight the impact that choices in any of these areas could make. Clear goals will empower you to have better clarity on the consequences of making the wrong decision. Too many young adults live by the mantra 'you only live once' and sure, this may be true, but the choices you make at 20 years of age could impact you for another 80 years!

Clearly, there is also a place for everyone to learn from their mistakes and not always be 'sheltered' from making your own mistakes. We can all reflect back on errors of judgment that we have made throughout life that have taught us lifelong lessons, and that's really important. It shapes the people we are, the personalities we have and our outlook on life. There are naturally people that are more dispositioned towards risk-taking and others that might shy away from confrontational situations. Our brains are all uniquely wired, and that's the beauty of the human species. Life on earth for humans wouldn't have lasted long if we all thought the same, acted the same and said the same things!

Momentum
The choices we make regarding those friends and associates we choose to spend time with is one of those decisions that can also act as an anchor or sail towards the 'future you'. Friends that display little aspirations for doing great things complain all the

time, regularly make poor decisions on their health and wellbeing, don't treat people with respect and aren't supportive of you will essentially become an 'anchor' for your journey. In other words, they will hold you back from exploring the open waters of the world.

To the contrary, if you choose to spend time with friends that are positive, exciting, have a great outlook on life, that are in your corner, supporting you and inspiring you to achieve your goals, then you will be in the top 10%. These people will act as your sails on your journey, taking you out of the safe waters to open you up to a world of opportunities and excitement.

You may have developed friends as neighbors, through sport, school, work, college, vacations or other means, and those friendships may extend back a long way. Make sure you choose to be friends with great people, and you will open yourself up to great adventures and growth by connection. Choose to be friends with energy-drainers, and you can appreciate the path this will take you on; your road to success may take you to a dead end. As they say, you are the average of the five people you spend the majority of time with. If you look at it closely, they probably earn within 10 % of you, and they weigh 5-10kg either side of you and your values are all closely aligned.

Don't Wait – Take a Step and Fall Forward.

There are so many opportunities that are literally at your fingertips if you are prepared to just take that first step. Can you imagine if some of the world's best inventors, explorers, leaders or writers were not prepared to take that first step? Our life would be extremely different and things we take for granted today – such as the light globe, the smartphone, air travel or the computer – would not be around.

With any new journey, there's going to be a point where you need to take that first step. That step could be daunting, but it could also be an opportunity to completely change your life for the better. It's not going to be the steps you have taken that you regret, it's going to be the ones that you didn't take that will haunt you later on in life. Personally, I'd rather know that I tried and failed than to have not tried at all. If you were to meet two people and one had tried five businesses and had failed, while the second person had always promised to try something but never had, which person would you respect more? Which person would be more interesting to talk to about their experiences? Which person are you going to learn more from? It's clear: person number ONE!

This person can talk from experience about what they tried, what lessons they learnt, or what they would do differently from the other five businesses that haven't worked out. What interest would you have in the other person? Not much, because they have no business lessons to share, no experiences they can impart and they have never had the courage to start.

Some people think that to take that first step, you may need to take big risks, but that's not the case at all. Some may even be concerned about what others may think if they fail. Taking the first step towards a personal goal, a new relationship, or starting a new business, for example, can often provide amazing opportunities to gain knowledge, experience and different skills. Many find that once the first step is taken, the second step becomes easier as you start to gain momentum. Think of it like trying to push a stationary car. The first ten steps are often the hardest, and as you use significant force and energy to create forward momentum, the car starts to gather momentum. Your steps become longer, the force you apply decreases, and by step 20, the force required to push has significantly reduced.

If you are not prepared to put in the work and the energy to create the forward momentum to start with, things will always feel like you have the handbrake on. Too many give up in the early stages because things are 'too hard'. It's like trying to get the car rolling after three steps and quitting because it's not going fast enough. You may only be five more steps away from gaining the required momentum, but this is never realized as people quit too early. If you start by taking the first step, with the understanding that the initial push is the hardest, you will be better prepared for the initial tough stages of your journey.

MASTER SUCCESS

PRINCIPLE #9

HEALTHY MIND

HEALTHY BODY

Sustainability is Connected with Enjoyment

For many years, I was a physical education and sports teacher, and it was incredibly rewarding. I was fortunate to be in a position to positively impact many of my students and to educate them on the importance of regular exercise and maintaining a healthy diet.

With any kind of activity, it's so important to make the activity memorable and enjoyable, so over the years, I came up with my own acronym called E.S.C.A.P.E so it could help people identify what activity would be best suited to them.

E = Enjoyable

Whatever you choose, the activity must be enjoyable for you. There's no point swimming lap after lap in the pool if you don't enjoy the activity. Don't get talked into long-term gym memberships without first completing a two-month trial. During the trial, you need to commit fully to the activity, so you can get an appreciation for the enjoyment and commitment required.

S = Sustainable

I see no value in starting a training program or 'boot

camp' if it can't be sustained for a minimum of 12 months, or even more as you get older. I see too many people try and take up activities that they won't be able to maintain. Some body types are just more suited to different activities, so heed my warning at your own risk. For example, I see too many people with the wrong body type take on marathons. You need to be light and lean; otherwise, you will risk injuries to your ankles, shins, knees and lower back covering those significant distances. Running is fantastic as long as you have the appropriate footwear; don't cover huge distances in one go; allow your body to rest and repair; and run on surfaces that assist with the impact absorption, like grass or athletic tracks.

Low-impact activities such as golf, swimming, power-walking or cycling are excellent activities that don't have the impact on your joint capsules that running would. Degenerative activities can cause long-term injuries, which can have a long-term consequence on your capacity to perform later on in life. What you must avoid are activities that could cause injury through significant stress, because you will end up being out of the activity for weeks, potentially months if you sustain something serious and that will be detrimental to your overall fitness and sometimes mental health.

C = Convenient

If it takes a significant amount of effort to participate in your activity, you will usually find that your motivation will wane. For example, if you love to surf, but the beach is 45 minutes' drive each way, you need one-and-a-half hours just for travel. Also, if it takes a lot of setting up and packing down, then that can also be a motivation killer.

A = Active

With any form of exercise, you need to raise your heart rate to get some solid benefit out of the activity. Even if you walk, try and incorporate some hills and really 'power' along. Don't just dawdle along like you are on your way to the shops. It's great for your cardiovascular system to place small amounts of stress on your body, to get your lungs burning and your heart pumping as long as you tailor your activities for your age, medical conditions and current health.

P = Partner

If you can participate in an exercise that permits a partner to join you, it will certainly help with the enjoyment and motivation aspect. You don't need to have someone with you on every occasion, but activities that don't permit this can be very isolating.

E = Economical

You don't want your activity to be too costly. Equipment costs, entry costs or annual membership costs can eventually impact what activities or exercise you can participate in. You don't want your fitness dictated with what's happening in the hip pocket, but also don't be so tight that you are not able to participate in the activities that give you lots of pleasure. Remember, exercise is an investment in not only your physical health but your mental health, so consider the options that will be best for your fitness and social life.

Body Fuel

When the word 'diet' is raised, it conjures up an image of a serious weight-loss program, drinking a spinach smoothie, followed by a one-hour exercise video involving a young and highly energetic aerobics instructor.

Like exercise, your ultimate aim is to ensure your diet is sustainable and you don't jump from one fad to another. In its simplest form, 'INPUT VS OUTPUT = BALANCE'.

If you have a proportionately balanced diet that enables the food you consume to be burnt up on a day-to-day basis, then you maintain homeostasis or equilibrium. Some days, the energy you consume maybe a little higher, other days a little lower. But overall, as long as it balances out, you will maintain a healthy weight proportionate to your height and body type. If your input of food is higher than your output of energy, you will naturally gain weight, and your body will store it around your hips, thighs, arms, stomach, glutes and internal organs. If your output is higher than your input, you will also naturally lose weight. The problem is, some people use an increase in exercise as an excuse to increase their food intake when trying to reduce weight, and they wonder why nothing changes!

The simple formula of 'INPUT VS OUTPUT = BALANCE' is a starting point for you. You don't need to have a Bachelor of Physical Education or be a qualified nutritionist to understand the formula, but you do need to be self-educated on the food that you are consuming and to take careful note of what food, chemicals, toxins, additives and fluid enters your body. If you are consuming a lot of processed, high-sugar food with high levels of saturated fat, then you will balloon out and increase your risk of cardiovascular disease. Please don't be tempted to be caught up in the myriad of diet 'fads' that we hear about all the time. Personally, I think the worst one I'm hearing about is the 'high fat' diet that has been circulating. This diet even encourages people to be eating the fat layer off steaks that you would traditionally cut off. There's a reason that cavemen and cavewomen died young and it wasn't always to do with wild animals eating them!

The acronym of K.I.S.S (Keep It Simple Stupid) sums up a balanced diet well. Just make sure you eat lots of fresh vegetables of different colours (e.g. carrots, legumes, avocado, capsicum); have a couple of serves of fruit a day (variety is key); have a serve of fish each week; a couple of lean serves of meat (red and white); limit servings of high-carbohydrate foods such as bread and pastas; limit high-processed foods and foods containing sugar; have small servings of dairy each day (milk or yoghurt); include a handful of nuts each day, and drink 2-3 liters of water. Phew, I think I need a breath after that sentence! This is just a very, very basic list of the essentials that should make up 90% of your diet. Why 90%? Well, the remaining 10% can be set aside for an occasional indulgence, and I don't mean that you purchase a tub of ice-cream and pig-out! An ice-cream in a cone or small cup on the weekend is fine, a pizza every few weeks is fine too, and a small chocolate bar is okay. Just be sensible and have some 'self-control' when eating the 'indulgent' foods.

Conclusion

Now, I'm sure you have been taking plenty of great notes, completing the assignment and action tasks, but if not, we will 'reconnect the dots' and take a look back at some of the key Master Success Principles.

MASTER SUCCESS PRINCIPLE #1
Visualization is an amazing way to bridge the current with the future and best of all; you just need to close your eyes! The visualization process is a powerful way to awaken the subconscious mind as you bring your goals and ambitions to life. It's a very successful technique that when used well, creates pictures, moments and feelings that draw you closer towards the opportunities that you may previously have missed.

GOAL SETTING

STEP 1. CLARITY

DREAM BIG and stretch yourself. Get clarity on what you want.

STEP 2. PERSONAL

Make it personal and relevant to you

STEP 3. TAKE ACTION

Take immediate action and write up your BIG goals

STEP 4. PLAN

Develop your plan and course of actions steps

STEP 5. TIME

Develop specific and realistic time frames for your goals

STEP 6. COMMITMENT

Follow through with your commitment and start

STEP. 7 OPPORTUNITY

Be observant of opportunities that will present themselves

STEP 8. START

Do not procrastinate. Get stated today.

A really important area that we covered was regarding 'opportunity'. When you become more aware of the opportunity through the goal-setting process, you can suddenly see things in a new light.

It's almost like in *The Wizard of Oz*, the classic 1940 movie, when the movie screen transforms from black and white to color. You start to see things that you may have previously missed or walked straight past. Opportunities are constantly presenting themselves and in many different forms. It's your role to seize those opportunities in life because you never know where they may lead you.

MASTER SUCCESS PRINCIPLE #2

It's not just about the dreaming, it's not just about the writing, it's not just about your mindset, and it's not just about the visualization – it's a combination of all the above. In this chapter, we talked about the importance of thinking big but keeping in check what is possible vs. the impossible. You have an amazing opportunity to project your mind forward and to see how life could be different by using visualization.

We also talked through the physical process of writing your goals down and not just keeping them in your mind. It's the lack of physical evidence and accountability – of having your goals literally in your face for 365 days of the year – that helps you to revisit and keep on track. Place your goals in physical locations you will see daily, as a consistent reminder of what you want to achieve. Circumstances do change, and although you need to have firm and structured goals, you need to permit some occasional changes in direction that need to be reflected in your goals and the changes in your life.

MASTER SUCCESS PRINCIPLE #3

The development and structure of your daily habits must be designed to move you closer to your goals each and every day. It starts with the development of your goals, as you need to have a powerful **REASON** and a purpose attached to your goals to drive your commitment, enthusiasm and motivation.

Print up your daily habits and place them where you can look at them daily.

Make it as easy as possible for you to maintain your daily habits and introduce them slowly.

Avoid at all costs missing your daily habits for more than two days in a row.

Start with tiny habits and grow them with time.

On your own unique journey, just remain focused on staying in your lane and don't be so concerned at the speed of others. It's important though to always lookout for the opportunity to push a little bit harder and out of your comfort zone. You don't want to be comfortable; you want to be sitting just outside of your comfort zone, so you are always growing, innovating, learning and adding value.

MASTER SUCCESS PRINCIPLE #4

The new generation, due to the rapid advancements in technology, is expecting immediate results. Prior to the development of Google, if you wanted to look up information for a school project, you needed to go to the library, look through plenty of books, then take a photocopy of the page of interest and transfer that info across to your project.

These days, you can bring the same information up with more than a million options in 0.42 seconds! Don't treat your life like a search engine and expect immediate results. You need to listen, learn and absorb new knowledge and build relationships.

We also covered the importance of celebration. Make sure you pause and reflect, even for a short time to enjoy the moment and 'smell the roses.'

MASTER SUCCESS PRINCIPLE #5

With any change in your life, there will be a level of sacrifice you will need to make, and this may be tiny, or perhaps substantial. Immediately, people may feel that sacrificing comes at a detrimental cost, but those sacrifices could even save your life! Perhaps it's a change to a healthier diet, exercising for 30 minutes rather than sleeping in, giving up smoking to avoid lung cancer or not working seven days a week so you can have more time with your children. Work out what you need to **stop, keep doing** and **start** in your life to achieve the goals you want.

There are 10 key pillars that will give you every opportunity to maintain a healthy mindset and all must flow from each other. They complement each other and in combination, they will turbo-boost your success and fulfilment, therefore leading to a healthy mindset.

One: Set your goals

Two: A healthy diet, daily exercise and the right amount of sleep

Three: Good daily habits

Four: Be grateful

Five: Love and appreciate your friends, family and

your community

Six: It's not what you are dealt with in life; it's how you deal with it

Seven: Positively impact others

Eight: Be kind to others

Nine: Invest in yourself and your wealth

Ten: Make each day count

MASTER SUCCESS PRINCIPLE #6

Fear shouldn't be avoided. In fact, fear should be embraced to keep pushing you to a level of discomfort. There are different forms of fear, the main two being the fear response (fight or flight) when your life is threatened and the other being a fear of failure, usually induced by your limiting beliefs. Don't allow fear to rule your world, rather use it as an energy source to push your limits to another level. Remember, everything you want is usually just on the other side of fear!

On many occasions, you will hear inner voice, telling you to 'stop this' and 'avoid doing that'. This mechanism was pre-programmed into our brains thousands of years ago to keep us alive, but these days it can really impact our ability to take on risks that aren't life-threatening but can be huge success-killers. Become really conscious of your self-talk and recognize when it's doing you more harm than good.

MASTER SUCCESS PRINCIPLE #7

Strong role models, mentors and leaders can significantly enhance your probability to achieve success. Seek out those that have reached the goals you desire and ask 'great questions.' As Tony Robins says *"Successful people ask better questions, and as a result, they get better answers."*

The best mentors are those that meet these specific criteria:

They are great people. They demonstrate great human qualities. These may include being friendly, open, honest, sincere, treating everyone with respect, leading by example, being generous, engaging in a healthy lifestyle, holding healthy relationships with others, or being positive and displaying habits that elevate them to the top 10 per cent.

Open to share. Provide you with honest answers regarding things that have worked well for them, along with failures that have made them stronger.

Have achieved things that you would like to achieve. Single out people that have achieved particular goals that you would like to achieve. Because we all strive to achieve different goals, no one person will have every goal you want to achieve, but they may have achieved one or a few of the goals that you aspire to.

Make you inspired. Your mentors must have the qualities to inspire you. Avoid individuals that have the 'glass half full' mentality. These people fall into the 90% rule. We're aiming for the top 10% of achievers.

MASTER SUCCESS PRINCIPLE #8

The choices we make lead to the steps we take and the future we ultimately live. Each day, we all make decisions that will impact our lives, and they may be micro-changes or significant momentum-changers that move us closer or further away from our goals. Decisions such as our friendship groups, career, fitness, health, lifestyle, sports, transport, travel, finances are just a start. Ultimately, the choice will be yours, so make the best decision you can with the information you have and if it's wrong, make a correction as fast as you can, learn from it and move on.

With every decision you make, you are building your success foundation. Your decisions will help build resilience, strength of character and confidence to deal with environmental factors that feel like they're always trying to destabilize you. Like a 100-year-old tree, the broader and stronger your foundation, the more resistance and strength you have to deal with problems as they arise.

Momentum is "the force that keeps an object moving or keeps an event developing after it has started". Therefore, to gain momentum, you first need to make your first decision and take that first action to make something happen. The opposite of momentum is inertia, which is defined as "a tendency to do nothing or to remain unchanged". In other words, this is procrastination. A decision either way, be that right or wrong, still causes momentum as you follow a particular direction. Take action, 'fall forward' and don't allow your limiting beliefs to put on the handbrake.

MASTER SUCCESS PRINCIPLE #9

There's a really important balance you need to maintain in order to lead a successful and fulfilling life, and taking care of your health and physical fitness is critical. In this lesson, we got out of the classroom and into our gym gear for some fresh air in the outdoors.

For long term sustainability of fitness and activity, consider using the **E.S.C.A.P.E** acronym.

E = Enjoyable

Whatever you choose, the activity must be enjoyable for you.

S = Sustainable

Be very mindful of activities that can't be sustained for a minimum of 12 months or even longer as you get older. You need to be careful of high-impact activities that can place your joints under significant duress.

C= Convenient

If it takes a significant amount of effort to participate in your activity, you will usually find that your motivation will wane. Make it simple, close in locality and at times that are suitable for your lifestyle.

A=Active

With any form of exercise, you need to raise your heart rate to get some solid benefit out of the activity. Even if you walk, try and incorporate some hills and really 'power' along. Don't just dawdle along like you are on your way to the shops.

P = Partner

If you can participate in an exercise that permits a partner to join you, it will certainly help with the enjoyment and motivation aspect.

E = Economical

You don't want your activity to be too costly. Equipment costs, entry costs or annual membership costs can eventually impact what activities or exercise you can participate in. You don't want your fitness dictated with what's happening in the hip pocket.

To maintain a balanced diet, the easiest formula to remember is '**INPUT VS OUTPUT = BALANCE**. Don't try and overcomplicate your diet and be careful of fad diets that could have a negative impact on your requirement to obtain the right balance of food sources essential for growth, repair and energy.

Final Note

From personal experience, it's not always easy to adapt to change and even harder to take a leap of faith into the unknown. I want you to believe in your capacity to do whatever you want and to take every opportunity in life, so one day you can reflect back and know you have left nothing in the tank. Remember, you won't ever dwell on the things you tried, but regret the opportunities you never seized. We've been given a moment in time, just a fraction of a second on our 4.5 billion-year-old planet, to live life on our terms. With the advancements of technology, there has never been a greater time to do so, and we are truly fortunate to live in a connected world; one where you can engage with someone face-to-face on the other side of the planet with the push of a button. We have greater access than ever before to knowledge, experiences, lessons and inspiring leaders that enable us to grow, develop and empower and our minds.

I hope you can really feel the energy created in the words of this book because as we say goodbye, I want you to remember that the *decisions you make and the actions you take will define your success*. All the very best on your journey......

Reviews

Thanks so much for reading this book! I greatly appreciate it.

My aim is to provide impactful and helpful information that will help as many people as possible. The way you can help and to positively impact others is by leaving a review thus in turn spreading the word so others can improve their lives. I read every review I get and it helps me to make improvements and also know if you found value in the book.

About the Author

Mark Dalton is a former Australian elite athlete, business coach, motivational speaker, qualified sporting coach and owner of a growing consultancy business to assist athletes and business executives & owners to achieve their ultimate goals.

He has dedicated the past 27 years to help others in personal development through his coaching, mentoring and resources and has a passion for empowering others to achieve their maximum potential.

Mark has a 10-year goal to author 5 books in Personal Motivation and has commenced his journey with Master Your Mind – Master Your Success.

Mark Dalton
Author

References

Inner Drive, (2019). *How do you actually develop a growth mindset?* Retrieved December 16, 2019, from https://blog.innerdrive.co.uk/how-do-you-actually-develop-growth-mindset

Shore, J. (2019). *The most important key to your success is goal clarity*. Retrieved December 16, 2019, from https://jeffshore.com/2017/10/know-key-success-goal-clarity/

Pavlina, S. (2009). *11 Ways to Gain Clarity*. Retrieved December 16, 2019, from https://www.stevepavlina.com/blog/2009/12/11-ways-to-gain-clarity/

Turner, M. (2016). *Commitment: Being committed to your goal(s)*. Retrieved December 17, 2019, from https://getresults.org.uk/commitment-being-committed-to-your-goals/

Ackerman, C. E., (2019). *What is gratitude and why is it so important?* Retrieved December 17, 2019, from https://positivepsychology.com/gratitude-appreciation/

Robinson, T. (2019). *This is what happens when you move out of the comfort zone.* Retrieved December 19, 2019, from https://www.lifehack.org/articles/communication/this-what-happens-when-you-move-out-your-comfort-zone.html